POWER!

POWER!

Black workers, their unions and the struggle for freedom in South Africa

Denis MacShane,
Martin Plaut, David Ward

South End Press

Copyright © 1984 Dennis MacShane, Martin Plaut, David
Ward

Copyrights are still required for book production in the
United States. However, in our case it is a disliked necessity.
Thus, any properly footnoted quotation of up to 500 squential
words may be used without permission, so long as the total
number of words quoted does not exceed 2000. For longer
quotations or for a greater number of total words, authors
should write for permission from the publisher.

ISBN: 0-89608-244-x paper
ISBN: 0-89608-246-8 cloth

Printed in Great Britain

Cover design: Dave King

South End Press/302 Columbus Ave/Boston MA 02116

Contents

Notes

1. Terminology

   a. South Africa's apartheid system divides the country's peoples into so-called population groups. A 1950 law assigns every person to one of the three groups: white, coloured and black. The coloured group is further divided into Indian and Asian groups. As is well known the Africans were the original inhabitants of South Africa; the whites arrived in two waves mainly from the Netherlands and Great Britain from the 17th century onwards though they have been augmented since 1945 by white immigration from continental Europe and from the rest of Africa. The coloureds are the descendants of mixed marriages and African-white relationships while the Asian population, mainly Indian, are descendants of those brought to South Africa as cheap labour by the British in the 19th century.

   For the purposes of this book we follow the usage of the workers in South Africa which is to refer in general terms to all workers who are not in the white population group as black. So when you read of "black" workers this often includes African, coloured and Asian workers. When it is necessary to draw a finer distinction the report refers to "African" to mean the descendants of the original inhabitants of South Africa, "coloured" in accordance with the definition above and "Indian" or "Asian", as appropriate.

   b. The apartheid system has also created a set of so-called "homelands" or "national states" or "independent republics" which the Pretoria régime claims are the territorial entities to which many Africans belong. So, for example, the so-called Republic of Transkei was set up under the Status of Transkei Act which declares that all those born in Transkei or directly descended from Transkeians or who have linguistic or cultural ties to the Xhosa or Sotho groups in the Transkei shall no longer be South African citizens. The four so-called "independent republics" are Transkei, Ciskei, Bophuthatswana, and Venda. The "national states" are KwaZulu, Gazankulu, Lebowa, Qwaqwa, Ndebele, and KaNgwane. In the old usage these were always referred to as "bantustans" and it is how most workers in South Africa refer to them now as few people outside government circles accept the claim that these areas are countries, nations, or states in any accepted sense of the word. Therefore, unless there is a specific need to draw a specific distinction this book will refer to the above ten areas as "bantustans".

2. Population
   The population is divided as follows:

African	*White*	*Coloured*	*Asian*
20.8 million	4.5 million	2.6 million	820,000

3. Government
   The ruling Nationalist Party has been in power since 1948. It currently enjoys a large majority in parliament. There is strong criticism of apartheid in the English language press.

4. Trade Union Federations and independent or emerging unions
   Chapter 3 provides more details but before then you will come across references to TUCSA, FOSATU and CUSA. TUCSA, the Trade Union Council of South Africa, was established in the 1950s and is white dominated though it has many black members. FOSATU, the Federation of South Africa Trade Unions was founded in 1979. It is non-racial. CUSA, the Council of South African Unions, was launched in 1980. Its philosophy is close to black consciousness. Other unions are not affiliated to any centre. Generally all the black-led non-TUCSA unions are labelled as independent or emerging.

5. Currency
   Most figures are quoted in Rand. In April 1984, R1 equalled £0.55 or US$0.80. The minimum wage in the metal industry in April 1984 was R1.53 an hour, ie: a monthly salary of R269 or £148 or $215. Prices in the shops for food, clothes, leisure were about the same as Western Europe or North America.

Abbreviations

South African Trade Union Federations, and their affiliates mentioned in this book.

CUSA: Council of Unions of South Africa
NUM: National Union of Mineworkers
FOSATU: Federation of South African Trade Unions
MAWU: Metal and Allied Workers Union
NAAWU: National Union of Automobile and Allied Workers Union
NUTW: National Union of Textile Workers
SACOL: South African Confederation of Labour
TUCSA: Trade Union Council of South Africa

Historic Unions and Federations

CNETU: Council of Non-European Trade Unions
FOFATUSA: Federation of Free Trade Unions of South Africa
ICU: Industrial and Commercial Workers Union
PTU: Progressive Trade Union Group
SACTU: South African Congress of Trade Unions

Unaffiliated black unions

CTMWA: Cape Town Municipal Workers Association
FCWU: Food and Canning Workers Union
GAWU: General and Allied Workers Union
GWU: General Workers Union
CCAWUSA: Commercial Catering and Allied Workers Union of
    South Africa
BMWU: Black Municipal Workers Union
MACWUSA: Motor Assembly and Component Workers Union of
    South Africa
SAAWU: South African Allied Workers Union
OVGWU: Orange Vaal General Workers Union

Political Organisations

ANC: African National Congress
PAC: Pan Africanist Congress
NFC: National Forum Committee
UDF: United Democratic Front

International Trade Union Federations and Secretariats

ICFTU: International Confederation of Free Trade Unions
WFTU: World Federation of Trade Unions
IMF: International Metalworkers Federation

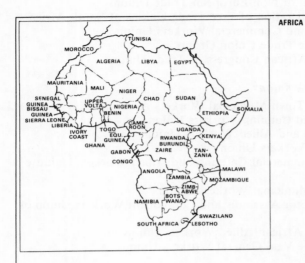

AFRICA

TUNISIA
MOROCCO
ALGERIA LIBYA EGYPT
MAURITANIA
MALI NIGER
SENEGAL UPPER CHAD SUDAN
GUINEA VOLTA
BISSAU NIGERIA
GUINEA BENIN ETHIOPIA SOMALIA
SIERRA LEONE CAME-
LIBERIA ROON
IVORY TOGO UGANDA
COAST EQU. RWANDA KENYA
GHANA GUINEA BURUNDI
GABON ZAIRE TAN-
CONGO ZANIA
ANGOLA MALAWI
ZAMBIA MOZAMBIQUE
ZIMB-
ABWE
NAMIBIA BOTS-
WANA
SWAZILAND
SOUTH AFRICA LESOTHO

SOUTH AFRICA — PRINCIPAL CITIES AND TOWNS

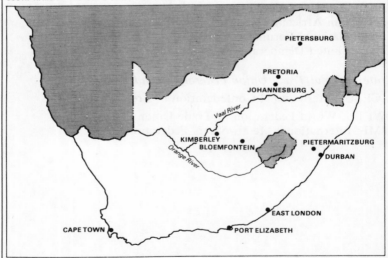

PIETERSBURG

PRETORIA
JOHANNESBURG

Vaal River

KIMBERLEY PIETERMARITZBURG
BLOEMFONTEIN DURBAN
Orange River

EAST LONDON

CAPE TOWN PORT ELIZABETH

Foreword

This short book is to explain to people outside South Africa the immense growth in trade unions organising black workers in that country. There are now more than 550,000 blacks organised in trade unions. On average there has been a strike a day in South Africa over the past three years. The apartheid state and the employers have had to come to terms with the growth of an organised working class. Clearly this has important implications for the struggle for democracy, political freedom and economic and social justice in South Africa. Workers and unions in countries outside South Africa can now play crucial roles in building solidarity with their brothers and sisters in South Africa. In this book we try to describe the growth of this black trade union movement, its fight against repression, its successes and its problems. We have not attempted to describe the full horror of the daily existence of 80 per cent of the South African population which is not white. The Carnegie Foundation has recently sponsored a major study into poverty in South Africa. Four hundred researchers from 20 South African universities have been at work since 1982. Their first findings which emerged in 1984 showed that one third of all black children under the age of 14 did not get enough food to eat and were stunted in their growth. In Cape Town, a nuclear power station came on stream in 1984, yet for most blacks the only heating source in one of the bantustans ('homelands') is firewood the people have to spend 150-million man-hours a year collecting. The pass laws and group areas Acts, which control where blacks live, work and travel are still in force. Since 1948, 12.5 million people have been arrested or prosecuted under the pass laws. In 1983, 140,000 violations of the various controls on movement or habitation were recorded, an average of nearly 400 a day. Since 1960, three-and-a-half million people have been forcibly evicted from their homes and a further two million are threatened.

The activities of the security police have been responsible for the deaths in custody of Steve Biko, Neil Aggett and many others. Nelson Mandela and other black leaders remain in prison. Discrimination is still visible in segregated transport, housing, beaches and lavatories. The wealth of the whites contrasts with the poverty of the blacks. Two important categories of workers — agricultural labourers and domestic servants, are not permitted to organise in a trade union. There is no evidence that the ruling white minority will give up or even lessen its control without a determined struggle.

We have not dwelt at length on these problems. They are well covered in reports, articles and books elsewhere. The excellent range of publications produced by the International Defence and Aid Fund or by the anti-apartheid movement provide fully documented evidence of the cruel and inhuman consequences of apartheid for the people of South Africa.

Nor have we written about the important and interesting political developments inside South Africa including the arrival of the United Democratic Front, the National Forum Committee, nor indeed about the activities of the African National Congress, nor about the political dynamic of Southern Africa as a whole including the Namibia conflict, the signing of a treaty with socialist Mozambique or the problems facing the Zimbabwe and Angola governments. The debate around what form of capitalist relationships exist in South Africa is a profound one which space does not permit us to enter. Nor to judge the value of the ideas of the black consciousness movement as opposed to those who argue for a class-based approach to the liberation of South Africa.

It may seem strange to list what a book does not cover but it is better at the outset to make clear that this book concentrates on the black working class and their unions. Although a great deal of material is available in South Africa on this subject very little has been published at length outside South Africa, and what does exist is often written from a narrow viewpoint aimed to boost the position of particular exiled organisations or specific political perspectives or party analyses.

Readers of the *South African Labour Bulletin* will see the immense debt we owe to its editors and contributors and we are grateful to its editors for permission to quote from its many articles. The *South African Labour Bulletin* is a model for a rigorous, yet accessible review of a country's trade union and labour movement scene. Anyone interested in what is happening to black workers and their organisations in South Africa should subscribe (SALB, 4 Melle House, 31 Melle Street, 2001 Braamfontein, South Africa). We have also drawn on the journals, bulletins and publications of the South African trade union movement and from personal interviews conducted in South African workplaces and townships in March 1984. Finally, one should note the contribution of some of South Africa's journalists who report labour news. Their coverage is first-rate and any student of the black trade union movement in South Africa will find plenty of material in the *Rand Daily Mail,* the *Financial Mail,* the *Star,* the *Argus,* the *Sowetan* and *City Press.*

The Trade Union International Research and Education Group at Ruskin College, Oxford has produced a video called 'The Workers Struggle in South Africa'. They showed it to a group of shop stewards in Manchester. One of the shop stewards said afterwards: "It wasn't the level of repression in South Africa shown in the programme that surprised me. I felt I knew about that already. It was the level of organisation among black workers, that I just didn't know was there. I didn't realise that such union organisation was possible there, much of it is fighting against British companies like our own."

This book is written for people like him. It is dedicated, however, to the workers of South Africa. They are engaged in a struggle whose outcome is far from certain. But in fighting for working class rights and building independent democratic workers' controlled unions they are setting an example to the world.

Denis MacShane, Martin Plaut, David Ward
July 1984

Chapter 1

Durban 1984, Durban 1973

Slowly, the workers came over the hill. From the township in Clermont where they lived to the industrial areas around Durban where they worked was a distance of 15 kilometers. It had meant getting up much earlier in the morning; it would mean not arriving home until well past nightfall. They walked cheerfully, singing songs and from time to time shouting out 'Amandla' — Power! — and punching the air with their fists. Every few minutes an empty bus would be driven quickly past the walking workers. Troops of police drove up and down the line, occasionally lobbing a tear gas grenade. It was 14 March 1984 and this was another episode in the long struggle for workers' rights in South Africa.

The dispute between 200 bus drivers and the Durban Transport Management Board will perhaps not even be mentioned when the future historians of the South Africa labour movement begin their work. It was over in a matter of days. There was little media interest. In any democratic country it would never have happened. Yet the Durban bus drivers' strike in March 1984 brought into play the following elements: a workplace occupation, mass dismissals, the hiring of strike-breakers, police charges and tear-gas attacks on innocent bystanders, a community boycott, the threat of a general strike in Durban, the winding up of a hated management controlled liaison committee, and a clear victory for workers, the community and their union.

The issue was simple enough. The 200 black drivers employed by the Durban Transport Management Board wanted their union, the Transport and General Workers Union, to be recognised as representing their rights and interests. They wanted to elect shop stewards and they wanted the management to talk with them rather than through a management-workers liaison committee whose composition was heavily weighted in favour of the Transport Board. As public employees they had no legal right to strike. They knew that many of their fellow trade unionists had achieved recognition in the textile and industrial plants in Durban. But municipal and state bodies, particularly those responsible for transportation had resisted efforts by the independent black unions to win recognition agreements.

Two years previously, further down the coast in Port Elizabeth,

800 workers employed by SATS, the state transportation company had gone on strike to win recognition for their union, the General Workers Union. The strike had been crushed, the workers dismissed and those who were migrants were forced back to their bantustans. Every municipal employee in South Africa was aware of the cruelty used against Johannesburg city council workers in 1980. So the Durban bus drivers were taking a risk when they decided to go on strike to press for union recognition.

The strike began on a Friday when the workers occupied the bus depot at Clermont. Over the weekend the management told them over loudspeakers that they should return to work and that they all faced dismissal. The management showered the workers with leaflets saying they could be charged under the Riotous Assemblies Act. In addition to its police, Durban has a specially trained municipal "combat group". Heavily armed with shotguns, they backed their vehicles into the yard where the workers were meeting and began swinging their batons in an attempt to intimidate the strikers. On Monday, the workers were told that they had been formally dismissed. Police arrived to evict them from the depot but the workers left peacefully. The Transport Board began hiring replacement drivers and also told inspectors to drive the buses. The workers took the struggle into the community. Union activists in other unions spread the word that no-one should use the buses to go to or from work. The police patrolled the columns of workers. Near the bus depot and a shopping centre the police suddenly ran amok, driving their Land Rovers straight at groups of passers-by and firing hundreds of tear gas grenades. On Wednesday, there was a general meeting of shop stewards from the unions in Durban in the FOSATU federation, to which the Transport and General Workers Union belonged and which is the most important of the independent, black-led union federations which has emerged in South Africa.

The shop stewards decided to send a delegation to the mayor of Durban. They also debated whether in addition to the bus boycott they would consider a protest stoppage in the Pinetown industrial area. The concept of "pressure" is one much bandied about in discussion of industrial disputes. Sometimes pressure can be directly measured in terms of production halted or revenue lost. Sometimes the desire to avoid a major confrontation on the part of employers, uncertain as to what its outcome might be, is a form of pressure that produces a settlement in favour of workers at an early stage. Employers in Durban must have asked themselves why on earth should they have to face the possibility of industrial action, not to mention the irritation of the bus boycott making workers tired on arrival at work yet at the same time emotionally charged

with the solidarity action they were engaged in, when the issue —
that of union recognition and the election of shop stewards was one
they had already conceded in their own factories? Similar points
were made in a debate in the Durban City Council and by
Thursday, six days after the strike had begun the Durban
Transportation Management Board was negotiating with the union
about recognition. By Thursday evening all the dismissed bus
drivers were reinstated, the liaison committee had been removed,
and in a written agreement the Board had accepted the election of
six shop stewards who would "have the right to represent members
in disciplinary and grievance hearings and will be afforded the
traditional facilities of such representatives." The management
also granted access to the bus depots for full-time union officials
and agreed to deduct union subscriptions at source if an employee
decided to join the union and forward the cash to the Transport
and General Workers Union.

Power in the workplace

For both the workers and their union it was an important victory.
Unions may have charismatic leaders or may figure large in the
media, but what counts for workers is to know that they are no
longer powerless in the workplace. A shop steward at Alusaf, one
of South Africa's aluminium companies put it this way: "Some
people used to bow when they see the white people saying 'Baas,
baas'. But we have changed that attitude now and everybody, if
he's a man, he's a man . . . They don't feel victims of another
nation now. Although they know that these people have got the
money, and are wealthy, the workers have managed to erase the
slave from themselves by not bowing to anybody."

Page 2225 of the Shorter Oxford English Dictionary tells us that
a Trade Union is: "An association of workers . . . for the
protection and furtherance of their interests in regard to wages,
hours and conditions of labour . . ." Yet the Durban bus drivers
were not striking for more money, shorter hours or better facilities
in the depot; no, their struggle had a wider political and social
significance. As with workers everywhere the act of forming a trade
union and having to overcome the hostility of the employers and
their agents, having to face off the threats of the police and ignore
the dismissal orders, having to learn to talk with each other and
take decisions collectively and democratically, all this added up to a
sense of regaining some control over their lives, a sense of control
that in South Africa had been doubly denied them as workers and
as blacks.

It was in Durban, 11 years previously that the first great wave of strikes began to hit South African industry giving birth to what is now a strongly-based, militant, democratic and still growing trade union movement composed almost entirely of black workers. In 1969, there were 13 african unions with 16,000 members. In 1973, about 40,000 black workers were organised in unions. Now 550,000 black workers are organised in industrial and general unions. The emerging unions have full-time organisers, offices in different regions of the country, employ specialist experts as health and safety officers, legal advisers, educationists and editors.

The independent trade unions have emerged as amongst the most coherent, best organised opponents of apartheid because they are slowly gaining the power to hurt the regime economically. Employers and pro-management academics have been desperately organising seminars on how to deal with black unions and launching appeals for unions to restrict themselves to economic issues and avoid political questions. This has been brushed aside by the black unions who have continually called for the introduction of political democracy, have denounced the apartheid infrastructure such as influx control and the Groups Areas Act, and have campaigned strongly against the 1983 constitution referendum which proposed to white voters the setting up of "parliaments" for coloureds and Indians while leaving africans disenfranchised.

The black National Union of Mineworkers, which since its founding by the Council of Unions of South Africa in 1982 has shot to a membership of 70,000, has a subtle, clever but cautious leadership. Whoever threatens the gold mines in South Africa, threatens not just the very foundation of South African wealth but menaces a key segment of white South Africa's sense of history and enduring control. The greatest strikes in 20th century South African history, involving both black and white workers, involved the gold mines. Political upheavals leading to key changes in government followed the great mining strikes that came after both world wars.

No single group of workers has seen so many of its leaders victimised. 95 per cent of the 600,000 black miners are migrant workers. Dismissal from the mine means a return to a bantustan. The president of the NUM, James Motlatsi, is a migrant worker from Lesotho. So for him and his colleagues the need to tread carefully in building up their union is paramount. An all-out strike by his members would be unlikely to end in a negotiated settlement, with one side winning or losing, gracefully or otherwise, and the strikers suffering privation for the duration of the dispute: in South Africa, a serious, completely engaged miners' strike at the present level of organisation and balance of forces would almost certainly involve repression, bloodshed and mass dismissals. Motlasi recalls a spontaneous strike in the Western Deep Levels mine in 1973. Anger over meagre wages exploded when managers told the black miners that they were unskilled men fit only to hack at the rockface with their picks. The workers decided to go on strike and went back to the hostels to urge their colleagues not to report for the next shift. Security forces moved in and the sight of fixed bayonets made the massing workers more angry. Someone threw a stone at the troops and others followed suit. The troops opened fire and 12 miners were killed.

Motlasi was 22 at the time but the memory stays inside him. With it is anger, but also an eye to maintain and extend organisation and to increase worker education before letting emotion spill over into a confrontation out of which the miners are unlikely to emerge as winners.

Politics comes in

Yet such a perspective does not make the NUM mealy mouthed or hesitant in its political analysis. Here is how the NUM uses simple and direct language in its handbook for shaft stewards:

"Employer	*Worker*
1. He has money;	He has no money that is why he needs a job;
2. He is white and enjoys the support of government;	He is Black and the government discriminates against him;
3. His main aim is to make a big profit out of the Worker;	His major aim is to make a living out of wages. He must work or his family will starve;
4. He usually knows more about the job than the worker;	May not fully know the job and how the company operates;
5. He has the power to employ and dismiss;	He has no powers or say in the workplace;
6. He is well educated and crafty;	He has had no schooling;
7. He can pick and choose his workers	Because of unemployment, he cannot choose employer.

From the above factors we therefore see that the worker is in a terribly weak position. His weak position will stay that way from the day he is hired to the day he is fired unless he does something about it. To get out of that position of weakness, workers need to form their own organisation so that they can turn their weakness into strength. When workers form a brotherhood they outweigh the might of the employer, they deal with him from a position of strength and not weakness."

A meeting held in March 1984 of metal unions in Johannesburg, which included major affiliates of both FOSATU and CUSA, adopted a resolution, in which the delegates noted "that the voice of the majority of the working people has been suppressed, their organisatons crushed and that their political rights are still being denied" and resolved "to continue to fight for the total liberation of workers and the development of majority trade unions as a vehicle for change."

There is an important debate (see Chapter 10) going on in the emerging unions about what should be their precise relationship with political bodies in South Africa such as the United Democratic Front, the National Forum Committee, AZAPO (the Azanian Peoples' Organisation) or even Inkatha, the KwaZulu based political organisation set up by Chief Buthelezi. Never officially mentioned is the clear support amongst many black workers for the African National Congress and especially for the imprisoned Nelson Mandela. As one Port Elizabeth shop steward put it: "We long for the day when there is majority rule government in South Africa and Nelson Mandela is our Prime Minister. But when that day comes we must have an independent trade union organisation to make sure the black workers don't get kicked around simply because our people are in power."

The building up of those unions has taken a decade of constant work since the Durban strikes in 1973. It has been a hard slog, punctuated by fierce internal debate about the nature and role of trades unionism, the relationship of the black working class to capital and the apartheid state, and, in particular, important and difficult strategic and tactical decisions to be taken about such issues as the role of whites in the emerging unions, the ratio of recruitment to education and organisation, the use of labour law, the acceptance or refusal of government registration and whether to join the employer dominated Industrial Council system. There have been divisions between unions following the black consciousness line and those that argue that non-racialism should be a guiding principle. Inevitably, there have been personality clashes and differences of opinion about whether forceful leadership offered by an individual encourages workers' confidence or whether a personality cult and over-dominance of a union results. The balance between the power of full-time officials and that of the rank and file membership of an executive committee remains a problem. Organising unions on a national basis has been difficult. South Africa is five times the size of Great Britain. Cape Town is 1,000 miles from Pretoria. The economy, racial composition, and political and industrial history of the Western Cape is very different from Transvaal. Unions have grown up based on different industrial areas and there is considerable autonomy, not to say rivalry, between branches of unions covering different provinces. As we shall see later there have been major steps taken towards a greater degree of trade union unity. The differentiation in union development and outlook has naturally been a source of weakness. But it has also permitted the emerging unions to develop at their own pace and to seek out members and confront employers in a wide variety of ways. A monolithic aproach to organisation, negotiation and confrontation would have presented employers and the state with a single target, readily identified and hence more easily dealt with.

The 1973 strikes in Durban

All these problems were far from the minds of the strikers in Durban in 1973. In the 10 years leading up to those strikes there had been little industrial activity by black workers. The repression of the South African Congress of Trade Unions (SACTU) in the early 1960s and the indifference of the Trade Union Council of South Africa (TUCSA) to the needs of black workers meant that there was no leadership or trade union expression given to the rising tide of black industrial discontent. The following table shows the number of strikes by black workers 1962-1972.

Strikes by black workers: 1962-72

Year	No. of Disputes	Black workers on strike
1962	56	2,155
1963	61	3,101
1964	99	4,369
1965	84	3,540
1966	98	3,253
1967	76	2,874
1968	56	1,705
1969	78	4,232
1970	76	3,303
1971	69	4,196
1972	71	8,814

During this period of labour quiescence, the South African economy was expanding at a rate matched only by that of Japan. Between 1960 and 1970 it grew by 56 per cent. Foreign investment increased from R1819 million to R3943 million. But black workers, who by 1970 formed 78 per cent of the workforce in the manufacturing and construction sector, and 90 per cent in the mining sector, were not sharing in this bonanza of rapidly increasing industrial development, nor in the sharp upturn in South Africa's national income following the increase in the price of gold after President Nixon suspended dollar convertibility in 1971. A devaluation of the rand by 8 per cent in 1971 combined with an increase in world food prices meant that between 1971 and 1973 there was an increase of 40 per cent in the poverty datum line — the minimum subsistence level. Bus fares increased by 16 per cent. There was also mounting unemployment. Between 1961 and 1979 unemployment went up by 4,000 a month; between 1971 and 1975, the rate of increase in joblessness was 11,000 a month. In 1973, a survey showed that 80 per cent of the African employees in British and South African controlled firms were paid below the Poverty Datum Line.

These problems were accutely felt in Durban, where 165,000 African workers constituted one of the largest group of industrial workers in South Africa. The major industries are garment, textile, general engineering, food processing and tyres (Dunlop). The factories are generally small, single storey affairs. In January 1973, a strike began in a brickworks. 2,000 workers went on strike for higher wages. They marched down the streets, chanting: "Man is dead, but his spirit still lives." They won a wage increase. The strikes spread to factories belonging to the Frame group, South Africa's largest textile employer and notorious for low wages and poor conditions. Before the end of January, some 6,000 Frame employees were on strike. They obtained relatively modest wage increases. But the strikes moved on like a wave. As one factory won a wage increase and returned to work, another group of workers would come out on strike. The Durban press gave the strikes considerable publicity and word spread quickly in the townships. According to one observer: "Typically, the stoppages seem to have followed spontaneous mass meetings at the workplace; wage demands were not normally specified at the outset, but once formulated these involved ambitious increases. Serious bargaining did not occur, for no worker representatives were prepared to come forward and risk victimisation. Commonly the employers offered increases of up to £2 a week which, though usually rejected initially at mass meetings, were normally accepted when it was clear that no further improvements were forthcoming."

Help from "outsiders"

By the end of 1973, about 100,000 workers in Durban had gone on strike. Strikes also hit other industrial centres elsewhere in South Africa, but Durban was the focal point for the 1973 strike wave. Employers and the government were aghast. The strike wave appeared to have come from nowhere. Its spontaneity was undeniable but effective. But widespread industrial action still requires some organisation and leadership. The year before, 1972, there had been a successful strike by bus drivers in Johannesburg. 300 had been arrested after a sit-in but their services were needed for the daily transport of 120,000 black workers. In the end they won wage increases of 35 per cent. In addition, white students and post-graduate researchers who had been active in the radical students union offered their services as advisers to black workers. The great era of student and young intellectuals' political radicalisation associated with the events of 1968 in France, with the anti-Vietnam war campaign in the United States, the Prague spring in Czechoslovakia, the university demonstrations in Warsaw, the student revolts in Britain, the hot summer (1969) in Italy, also had its effect in South Africa where young white, usually English speaking would-be political activists could not help but be influenced by this worldwide movement of ideas. Outright left-wing activity of a political party nature was impossible in South Africa: however, one of the main ideas to emerge from the 1968 movement was that of the industrial working class as the major agent of political progress and dynamic change. In Natal, the National Union of South African Students had formed a "Wages Commission" which exposed the poor living standards of african workers. Young whites associated with the "Wages Commission" were active in helping strikers in Durban in 1973. The exclusively black South African Students Organisation had been founded in 1969; the Black People's Convention was launched in 1972 together with a general workers' union, the Black Allied Workers Union. What became known as the black consciousness movement was beginning to be active at the time of the Durban strikes. Finally, there was the behind-the-scenes involvement of older generations of workers who had been activists in the war-time and post-war period of industrial action under the Council for Non-European Trade Unions or later in the 1950s with SACTU. Although many key activists were arrested, imprisoned or forced into exile, there were also hundreds, possibly thousands, who had a living experience of union organisation and agitation which would once again be put to use. Veteran trade union leaders like Oskar Mpetha and Morris Kagan who had managed, just, to keep legally functioning as trade union officers were to be a source of advice and encouragement to the emerging unions. The Durban strikes also gave an impetus to the handful of coloured and Indian trade union officials who worked for TUCSA but resented TUCSA's indifference to African workers. Some of them left to form a car-workers' union which in due course would become one of the best-run and most militant of the FOSATU unions.

The wage levels against which the Durban strikers were protesting were extremely low, often less than R15 a week. Employers found that they could offer increases without much dent being made in their profits. The strikes were also embarrassing for foreign companies. American and European firms were suddenly and publicly exposed as paying wages which to public opinion in their own countries might seem little better than slave rates. The successful sporting boycott of South Africa had increased the country's sense of isolation and its need to cultivate its image as part of the Western community. Partly by skilful tactics involving staying inside workplaces for meetings, by not having any identifiable leaders, and avoiding major public demonstrations and partly by the short, sharp nature of the strikes the 1973 strikers avoided brutal police repression. Only 0.2 per cent of the strikers were prosecuted.

In short, both the employers and the state looked up at the end of the 1973 strikes and could see that it appeared that it was possible to live with black working class pressure, go through strikes, grant wage increases and yet survive. The power of the state, the authority of the employers, the strength of the economy appeared unscathed.

Reform, revolution, or repression are the three "r's" that 20th century capitalism has responded with when confronted with pressure from an organised working class. They are not necessarily three separate alternatives; as often as not repression has been found accompanying both reform and revolution. In South Africa, workers and their unions are still more aware of repression than reform. Yet after the Durban strikes the state and many employers opted, under growing and sustained pressure from black workers, for changes that amounted to a massive reform of labour law and employer-employee relations. The object of those trying to implement reform from on high was clear — in return for being granted a handful of rights that were supposed to approximate those achieved by unions in advanced capitalist countries the black workers would be grateful, content even. Instead the black working class has watched as the door has been opened inch by inch and each time kicked it a good deal further ajar. The process is far from over. But to understand the relationship between the strikes of 1973 in Durban and the 1984 strike for recognition by the Transport and General Workers Union in the same city we should first look in more detail at the South African economy, its system of industrial relations and collective bargaining, the changes in labour legislation following the 1973 strikes, and the history of black workers' struggles to form their own unions and negotiate with employers and the state.

Chapter 2

The History of Black Workers and their Unions

Black workers in South Africa have a long history of organising to improve their standard of living and to gain elementary trade union rights. Their history is a story of both bravery and a fierce determination to fight for "a better tomorrow", as one worker put it recently. But it is also the story of tragic reverses. For black workers have had to fight not only against a management that was as determined as any in the world to resist their demands, but also against a state uniquely organised along racist lines to deny blacks any say over their own lives. For this reason the democratic channels that played an important part for the working class in much of the developed world in its historical development, played little role in the emergence of forms of organisation amongst black workers in South Africa. Indeed, the entire weight of the state was at crucial moments utilised to break their trade unions and the political parties that sought at different junctures to assist the unions in their development. But there is also one further strand that cannot be ignored in any attempt to explain the emergence of unionisation in South Africa, and that is the disunity and fragmentation that has plagued the organisation of workers down the years. Sometimes on political grounds, and at others on racial grounds, black workers have for decades been weakened by the divisions in their own ranks. These three factors — determination, oppression and division, are central to the emergence of organisation amongst black workers. They are the central themes that dominate the story of the period. For in the last 60 years there have been at least four waves of unionisation that have washed over South Africa. Each has broken, or been broken, except the last. Each has left its mark and contributed to the struggles that have succeeded it, for although much is lost when a union is destroyed, lessons have been learned, and many workers recall their pasts with exceptional clarity. Perhaps the bitterness of the disputes brands these experiences on their memories.

Two other factors should be borne in mind in considering the growth of unionisation over this period. In the last 100 years South Africa has experienced massive industrial development. Since the discovery of gold and diamonds in the last quarter of the 19th century, the country's industrial wealth has been generated on a scale unknown elsewhere in Africa. In the period after the First World War much of this wealth was diverted by government action into the industrialisation of South Africa, to free it from its dependence on foreign manufacture. The giant Iron and Steel Corporation was only one of many state owned companies established in this period. Between the end of the First World War and the beginning of the Second, manufacturing grew from 10 per cent of National Income to 18 per cent. The Second World War saw a further increase in manufacturing and this trend was to be continued in the post-war years, and especially during the boom of the 1960s. Thus in 100 years South Africa has developed from being an agricultural colony of little importance on the world stage, through a massive development programme based on the mineral wealth of the country, to its current position as the most advanced industrial power on the African continent, with a diversified economy which boasts both a mining and a manufacturing sector that has placed the country amongst the ranks of the second order economic powers of the world. Clearly, this dramatic development has not simply been responsible for moulding the black worker, but has brought black workers to the centre of the country's development. For without their skills and sweat South Africa could not have developed in the way in which it has. It has also created a dual dependence of workers on management, but also of management on their workforce. One of the key reasons for the growth and success of the current trade union movement has been the increasing importance of black workers, both skilled and unskilled, to every sector of the economy.

And this brings us to the second area that, although crucial, will only be referred to in passing. That is the role of white workers and their political organisations. For as blacks have become increasingly important to the economy, white workers have declined in importance. Today the vast majority of whites are in highly skilled positions, or else in management. There are very few whites who today do not exercise some supervisory function over blacks. The last 100 years has been marked by the struggles of white workers to resist their gradual replacement by blacks, and the development of both white unionisation and the political parties that have represented white workers, leading to the victory of the Nationalist Party in 1948, can at least in part be traced to this defensive role.

The 1920s and the ICU

The first recorded instance of a strike by black workers occurred in

Cape Town as early as 1854, when the dockers struck for an improvement in their wages. But it was really in the aftermath of the First World War that organisation amongst blacks began. Strikes broke out amongst dockers and municipal workers, and in 1920 a massive strike by 71,000 black mineworkers took place. It was against this background of militancy that the first attempt at unionisation took place with the formation in 1919 of the Industrial and Commercial Workers Union — the ICU.

The ICU, founded by the Malawian (then Nyasaland) schoolteacher, Clements Kadalie, grew rapidly as a result of a successful strike on the Cape Town docks. In an atmosphere in which blacks felt themselves to be both powerless and oppressed, the ICU appeared as a beacon of hope. As the London *Times* put it: "The genuine grievances of the South African Natives provided the hotbed in which the ICU flourished. Rack rented Natives in the urban locations, underpaid Natives in Government employ, badly treated Natives on European farms, flocked to join the movement." As the report indicates, the ICU, which rapidly spread from its base in Cape Town to the Cape ports of East London and Port Elizabeth, then to the Orange Free State and the Transvaal, became a focus for a wide range of grievances, and soon took on the character of a mass movement rather than a trade union. The ICU's chief weakness was also one of its strengths — Kadalie himself. While Kadalie was both a charismatic and flamboyant figure, he was a poor administrator and organiser. The result was that the organisation grew with extraordinary speed, but lacked any coherent structure. This was exemplified by the area of the ICU's greatest expansion — rural Natal and the eastern Transvaal. Here, blacks deprived of land by the notorious 1913 Land Act were being squeezed off the land on which they squatted by white farmers keen to transform their holdings into modern farms. In their desperation they joined the ICU in their thousands. But although the ICU expanded with enormous rapidity, reaching a peak of 100,000 members in 1927, it was a highly unstable organisation, and rapidly crumbled. The dissolution of the ICU was hastened by fierce disputes within the organisation about the role of the South African Communist Party, which was formed in 1921, and tried to gain influence in the ICU.

The Communist Party had supported the white miners' strike in 1922 and coined the slogan: "Workers of the World Unite and Fight for a White South Africa". The difficulties were exacerbated when in June 1927 Kadalie left on a triumphal tour of Europe that lasted until November, leaving the organisation without leadership in a crucial period. On his return, Kadalie attempted to introduce long overdue organisational reforms, but the union was beset by splits and workers drifted away from the organisation. The ICU ran into financial difficulties and in 1928 a number of branches broke away from the organisation. By the following year the ICU had to all intents and purposes ceased to exist.

The 1930s and the Second World War

The collapse of the ICU did not spell the end of black unionisation. Its decline was in part responsible for a growth in the small, but important industrial unions that had sprung up, especially on the Witwatersrand. Their existence had come about because of the conflicts inside the ICU over the role of the Communist Party, which after December 1926 decided that "no officer of the ICU shall be a member of the Communist Party". Denied the opportunity of organising within the ICU, the Communists set up independent industrial unions. In 1928 five black unions with a combined membership of about 10,000 drawn from furniture and clothing factories, bakeries, laundries and garages founded the South African Federation of Non-European Trade Unions under a leadership consisting of Communist Party members.

The foundation of the Federation could not have taken place at a more difficult time. Not only was the country in the depression that was affecting the industrialised world, but it was faced with a government that was determined to break the power of black workers. The government saw this as being essential if it was to secure its objective — the replacement of black workers by whites as a way of eliminating unemployment amongst whites. The "poor white problem", as it was termed, had meant that one-fifth of all whites — some 400,000 people — were living in dire poverty. In order to remedy this situation the government turned on blacks. The notorious Minister of Justice, Oswald Pirow, told white workers that it was up to them to ensure that "public opinion declare it to be a disgrace to employ a native where a white man could be employed". Accordingly, a number of repressive laws were enacted, and the police were instructed to crack down upon the black unions with all the power at their command. Meetings were broken up and the premises of the unions attacked. Despite this campaign, the unions did have their successes. For example, in 1929 they were able to claim a "real breakthrough" when in the laundry trade a white union was persuaded to form a joint committee with a black union in an attempt to win better conditions for their members. But despite these isolated successes, the union movement was unable to sustain its position. Only the economic upturn that occurred just prior to the war brought a real increase in the power of black workers.

The end of the depression saw workers returning to the factories. The number employed in manufacturing alone rose by 58 per cent between 1932-33 and 1935-36. With the outbreak of war this trend increased sharply, and was further enhanced for black workers when a large number of whites enlisted in the armed forces, and created a shortage of labour. Between 1939 and the end of the war in 1945 the number of black workers in factories rose from 143,000 to 249,000. This increase in the demand for labour gave black workers the bargaining power that they had previously lacked, and their position was strengthened when, in November 1941, the small black unions came together to form the Council of Non-European Trade Unions (CNETU). The first president was Gana Makabeni, previously expelled from the Communist Party, but in 1945 he was to be succeeded by J.B. Marks, the chairman of the African Mineworkers Union, and a member of both the Communist Party and the African National Congress. Most strongly organised on the Witwatersrand, the Council had real strength in Port Elizabeth, Pretoria, East London, Cape Town, Bloemfontein and Kimberley. By the end of the war it was able to claim 119 unions as affiliates and a membership of 158,000.

The strength of the unions was built not only on the needs of the factories for labour, but also on the militancy of its members. In December 1942 a series of strikes broke out in Johannesburg, with 8,000 workers in the meat, dairy and brick industries going on strike. In Natal 400 coal miners walked out complaining about assaults from white foremen, insufficient food and long hours. Although the police reacted with their accustomed ferocity and 14 blacks were killed and 111 injured in Johannesburg, many of the strikes were successful. The Government, afraid that production badly needed for the war effort, would be affected, responded by allowing the Wage Boards, which were empowered to set wages across industries, to raise wage levels in a way unheard of before the war.

But perhaps the most significant advance was recorded in the mines where, for the first time, black workers were able to form unions. Again the stimuli were strikes that broke out in 1942 and 1943. The government established a commission of inquiry which recommended that since mineworkers had not had an increase in real terms for over 50 years, that their wages should be increased by a third. This was rejected by the mine owners, who only granted a small increase. Although most miners saw even this small increase as a victory, they were angered by the failure to implement the commission's findings.

But despite the obvious power that black workers could exercise, their union leaders failed to build on the gains that they had been able to make. In part this was the result of the political perspective of the Communist Party which, after the entry of the Soviet Union into the war, was determined that no action should be taken that would undermine the war effort. This position struck a chord with many in the movement, since black workers were only too keenly aware that the most reactionary elements in white society were backing a victory for fascism. Nonetheless, it meant that the early militancy of the workers was resisted by the union leadership, and workers were encouraged instead to take their cases to the Wage Boards set up by the government. This trend was opposed by some union members, and in 1944 the disagreements led to the formation within the CNETU of what was called the Progressive Trade Union Group. The PTU, led by Daniel Koza, argued that the workers had nothing to gain from assisting the government to win the war. Instead they called on workers to fight for better working conditions and greater worker control. For them the struggle was for socialism, not simply better working conditions. By 1945 they had been expelled from the CNETU and soon collapsed as a movement. These divisions, together with repressive measures that the government took as part of emergency war powers undermined the Council and meant that the unions emerged at the end of the war in a weakened position.

Despite its difficulties the CNETU was to lead one further major strike before it, too, was to collapse. This was the mineworkers strike of 1946. As was mentioned earlier, the mineworkers had not been satisfied by the results of the government commission. By 1944 the African Mineworkers Union had grown in influence, and claimed 25,000 members. In the following year post-war food shortages led to a deterioration in the standard of the food being provided in the mines, and at one mine in Johannesburg the miners went on a hungerstrike. At the union's annual conference in 1946 the union decided to ask for a minimum wage of 10 shillings a day, and other improvements in their conditions of employment. Its demands received only the briefest of replies from the Chamber of Mines, with a post-card informing the union that their demands were receiving attention. A wildcat strike broke out, and on 4 August the union held a special conference, at which the delegates passed a resolution warning the Chamber that if their intransigent attitude continued, a strike would be called from 12 August.

In adopting this position J.B. Marks warned the workers to expect violence, since, as he put it, "You are challenging the basis of the cheap labour system and must be ready to sacrifice in the struggle for the right to live as human beings." An old miner shouted out in reply: "We on the mines are dead men already".

And so the strike began. On the morning of 12 August between

60,000 and 70,000 miners stopped work in at least 12 mines. On the following day CNETU called a general strike in support, but the state confirmed Marks as correct and were determined to use any means to crush the dispute. Although the strike lasted a week, it was doomed. The police surrounded the compounds in which the miners lived, cutting them off from the outside world. Raids on the union's offices and arrests of the leadership limited the possibility of spreading the strike. Miners who attempted to resist by staging an underground sit-down strike were driven to the surface with brutality. Twelve were killed and 1,200 wounded. CNETU's attempts to provide support were broken by a massive police presence in the townships. By the 16th the strike was broken.

The result was not only catastrophic for the Mineworkers Union, which collapsed, but it fatally weakened the CNETU. In 1947, 22 of its affiliates seceded from the Council, citing as their reason the influence of communists in the leadership and the use of the strike weapon. Although CNETU struggled on, it was further undermined when, in 1950 the Communist Party was banned, and in 1953 the Council finally split up.

Unions against apartheid: the '50s and '60s

If the unions of the 1940s grew out of the war and the opportunities that it brought to black workers, then the unions of the '50s and '60s grew out of the increasing polarisation of South African society. For the period saw the triumph of Afrikaner nationalism in 1948, and its consolidation in the years that followed together with the unfolding of its policies of apartheid. For although racism had been central to white politics before, its institutionalisation in the post-war period with the election of the Nationalist Party on an overtly racist platform transformed the country's politics. A direct clash with the organisations representing blacks was inevitable. In such a climate workers became embroiled not only in clashes with management and the state, as they had in the years before, but became part of the pattern of resistance to apartheid. In later years commentators have chastised the union movement for subordinating the trade union struggle to the political battles of the day. In the prevailing climate there was little option, for blacks were in reality fighting for their political lives.

Amongst the legislation enacted by the Nationalist government was the Suppression of Communism Act of 1950. Not only did it ban the Communist Party, which disbanded itself, but it also removed a number of communists from the leadership of the union movement. In 1954 the government published a further bill — the Industrial Conciliation Amendment Act — which aimed at splitting the union movement along racial lines. It decreed that recogniton would not be granted to any union that had a multi-racial constitution, and required mixed unions to either split into uni-racial unions or else to set up separate racial branches, each with a white controlled executive. The move threw the movement into turmoil. The largest union body, the South African Trades and Labour Council (the predecessor to the present TUCSA) was deeply divided, since its affiliates had among its members Indians, coloureds and some Africans. At the same time it also organised white artisans, who were in favour of the new legislation. In October 1954 it arrived at what it hoped was a suitable compromise. Africans would be excluded from direct membership, and would instead become members of unions that would be represented on a liaison committee. Registered white unions in the same industry would then negotiate on their behalf. Nineteen unions refused to go along with this strategy, known as "parallelism". These included the Food and Canning Workers Union and the Textile Workers Industrial Union. Finally 14 unions broke away from the Trades and Labour Council and together with a rump of the CNETU unions formed the South African Congress of Trade Unions — SACTU. In March 1955 SACTU was born, with 19 affiliates and a membership of around 20,000.

SACTU was, from the first, not only non-racial (some 400 members of the laundry union were white) but political. The inclusion of the word "Congress" in its title signified its identification with the Congress opposition, of which the African National Congress was the most significant element. Its political character was reaffirmed at its first conference held in Cape Town in 1956. It then adopted the following declaration: "SACTU is conscious of the fact that the organising of the mass of workers for higher wages, better conditions of life and labour is inextricably bound up with a determined struggle for political rights and liberation from all oppressive laws and practices. It follows that a mere struggle for economic rights of all the workers without participation in the general struggle for political emancipation would condemn the trade union movement to uselessness and to a betrayal of the interest of the workers."

But although SACTU took a militant stand politically, and joined in the activities of the Congress alliance, of which it was a member from late 1955, it was first and foremost a trade union organisation. Its main strength lay in its local committees, which acted as a core, providing most of the financial and administrative support for its unions. At its inception SACTU's main support came from the Witwatersrand, with 15,000 of its members coming from this area. But as it grew its strength diversified. Its main fields of activity lay in manufacturing, food processing and services, but this left many areas untouched. Agriculture, transport and metals, as well as mining, which after the end of the African Mineworkers Union was almost unorganisable because of the strict security, were amongst the areas of the economy that were not successfully organised. Nonetheless the unions grew, despite much government hostility. By 1961 it had 35 unions and 53,000 members, of whom 38,791 were Africans. Most of this growth came as the result of campaigns to improve the workers' conditions of employment, and some unions were hastily brought together in response to strikes by workers in particular locations.

In its first two years of operation SACTU concentrated on building industrial unions, but after the Alexandra bus fare protests of 1957 in which workers resisted the increases in fares by walking to work en masse, the organisation switched its strategy to more broadly based campaigns. Early in 1957, 300 workers attended a "National Workers Conference" and resolved to press for a £1 a day minimum wage. The aim was not only to increase wages, but also to broaden the base of the movement to reach a wider audience. £1 a day committees were formed in all the major towns and won the support of the Congress alliance. On 26 June 1957, a stay at home — effectively a one-day general strike — was called as part of the Defiance Campaign being waged by the Congress Alliance against the laws being introduced by the Nationalist Government. The day drew support from many workers in Port Elizabeth and Johannesburg.

The following year a further stay away from work was planned on the slogans "£1 a day" and "the Nats must go". Called to coincide with the white elections, the campaign opened on 14 April 1958. This time it won only minority support, and was called off by the ANC national working committee after one day. A further three-day strike call was made in 1961, but again failed to draw the kind of response that the organisers had hoped, and was once again called off.

Again the unions were plagued by the kind of splits that had appeared in the past. In 1959, five unions formed the Federation of Free Trade Unions of South Africa, aligned to the Pan Africanist Congress, a movement which had grown out of the African National Congress and was the result of Africanists hostility to the influence of whites within the movement and, in particular with the role of the Communist Party. Although supported by the International Confederation of Free Trade Unions and TUCSA, FOFATUSA had little impact on the union scene beyond its main affiliate, the Garment Workers Union, led by Lucy Mvubelo, once an executive member of the SACTU.

But the main difficulty confronting SACTU was again the state. With the Sharpeville massacre of 1960, the government cracked down on all forms of opposition with unprecendented ferocity. The African National Congress and the Pan Africanist Congresses were banned, and under the wide ranging provisions of the 1962 Sabotage Act 160 members and leaders of SACTU were arrested between 1960 and 1966. By the middle of the decade SACTU had been effectively destroyed, despite the fact that it was never actually banned inside South Africa. Although one of its unions — the Food and Canning Workers — survived, and survives to this day, SACTU lost its presence in South Africa and followed the other members of the Congress movement into exile.

It has maintained itself in exile ever since, functioning in close liaison with the ANC. The exiled SACTU developed strong links with British and Canadian trade unions. The ruthless effectiveness of the security police in South Africa combined with penetration of many South African exile organisations has limited its capability to intervene industrially or organisationally amongst South African workers. Furthermore, SACTU is closely identified with the USSR dominated World Federation of Trade Unions (SACTU is still a WFTU affiliate) at a time when the most interesting and authentic working class drives for independent trade union organisation such as the metalworkers in Brazil, the copper workers in Chile or the Solidarity trade union in Poland were based on theories of workers' control at odds with the WFTU model which places the union firmly under the control of the state and its ruling party. The new generation of black workers' leaders and activists in South Africa have inevitably become more remote from the exiled SACTU organisation, though all acknowledged its historic role in the 1950s and the courage of its militants who had tried to keep the SACTU and hence the black trade unionists' flame alive in the 1960s.

Chapter 3

Unions in South Africa in the 1980s

The growth of black unions in the late 1970s and early 1980s has created a diverse and fluid labour movement in South Africa. The development of these independent unions has quickly created a new structure of trade union organisations and has placed heavy burdens on the old white-dominated labour movement.

Today the black independent unions inside South Africa are organised in two national confederations, the Federation of South African Trade Unions (FOSATU) and the Council of Unions of South Africa (CUSA). In addition there are a number of large, unaffiliated black unions, such as the South African Allied Workers Union and the General Workers' Union. Collectively these national centres and individual unions are frequently termed the "independent", "black", "non-racial", or "emerging" unions.

They must be sharply distinguished from the "white" or "multi-racial" unions.[1] The latter are organised in the remaining major trade union federations, the South African Confederation of Labour (whites only) and the Trade Union Council of South Africa (multi-racial).

SACOL

The South African Confederation of Labour (SACOL) is openly racist and exclusively composed of white unions. Recently SACOL has come into conflict with the South African government over its labour "reforms" and the decision to include black trade unions in the industrial relations system. In response to the Wiehahn Report of 1979, the Confederation's General Secretary warned the Minister of Manpower not to promote the erosion of the right of "our white labour organisations".

The most hardline of SACOL's affiliates is the Mine Workers' Union led by its General Secretary, Arrie Paulus. The MWU launched an unsuccessful strike against the Weihahn proposals in

---

1. In the South African context a distinction is drawn between non-racial and multi-racial organisations. The former demand a complete absence of any racial discrimination, whereas the latter implies a union that accepts all races but organises them separately.

1979 and has encouraged SACOL to adopt the role of defending the privileged position of white workers against the emerging independent and non-racial unions. The MWU has sought an alliance with the ultra-right-wing Herstigte (Purified) National Party (HNP) and Arrie Paulus has called on "all whites to join one union" to protect their jobs from black labour.

The major changes occurring in the South African labour movement are causing severe problems for SACOL. The confederation's hardline anti-reform posture has generated splits among affiliated unions. As a result SACOL has suffered a dramatic loss of membership from 240,000 members in 1980 to 120,000 in 1984. Most of the disaffiliated unions have departed from SACOL's ranks following changes in their constitutions to admit non-whites. For the future, SACOL is deepening its defensive strategy by launching a membership drive to draw in all unaffiliated unions with an exclusively white membership.

Union membership 1983

Africans	545,000 (1981 — 360,000)
Whites	488,000 (1981 — 468,000)
Coloureds and Asians	343,000 (1981 — 327,000)

Trade Union Federations in South Africa

Independent black and non-racial

Federation of South African Unions (FOSATU)	106,000
Council of Unions of South Africa (CUSA)	148,000

Multi-racial

Trade Union Confederation of South Africa (TUCSA)	446,000

Whites only

South African Confederation of Labour (SACOL)	126,000
Unaffiliated unions (various racial composition)	550,000

(*Source:* ILO Report on South Africa 1984)

TUCSA

The Trade Union Council of South Africa (TUCSA) is a multi-racial — as opposed to a non-racial — national centre. It was set up in 1954 and has long held an ambivalent attitude to organising black workers. TUCSA has at times expelled its black members so as to conform to government legislation, only to re-admit them later. This shifting policy changed in the 1970s when TUCSA allowed blacks to affiliate but only if organised in exclusively black unions, in parallel to the orginal unions which effectively "sponsor" them.

The so-called "parallel" unions are highly dependent on their parent unions for finance and administration. Many general secretaries of the parallel black unions are also the secretaries of the parent unions. Frequently they are introduced into a firm with the co-operation of the management in an attempt to head off the establishment of an independent union. For example parallel unions have been offered the use of company facilities denied to the independent unions.

The TUCSA General Secretary, Arthur Grobbelaar (who died in August 1984), has said that "the administration (of parallels) should continue to be subject to the overall supervision of the registered (white) union". Yet black workers have complained that subscriptions are deducted from their wages for a union they have never joined, which has no shop stewards and never holds meetings.

TUCSA affiliates have generally welcomed the legislation introduced post-Weihahn and have experienced little trouble in registering its parallel unions.

In the long term TUCSA seems to be in trouble. The independent unions like FOSATU and SAAWU etc., have gained shop floor credibility in contrast to the black parallels which are regarded with suspicion. At TUCSA's 27th annual conference in September 1981 delegates expressed deep fears about competition from the independent unions. "It cannot be denied", said a delegate, "that there is a terrific battle on the shopfloor, which extends to the townships, for the hearts and minds of South African workers". Revealingly conference delegates spoke bitterly about "so many people in responsible positions", including some government officials who describe TUCSA affiliates as "sweetheart unions".

Serving to highlight TUCSA's generally meek and subservient relationship with both industry and government has been the union's reliance on closed shop agreements to exclude recognition and deter membership of the independent unions. A classic example is in the textile industry where the TUCSA affiliated Garment Workers Industrial Union (GWIU) has enjoyed a dominant role courtesy of closed shop arrangements. The FOSATU affiliated National Union of Textile Workers (NUTW) has challenged the GWIU's monopoly and is taking legal action to defend its recognition claim. The NUTW gained recognition at the Pinetown clothing firm of James North following a ballot of the workforce. The clothing Industrial Council, however, refused to allow the workers to resign from the TUCSA union and rejected the NUTW's claim to introduce the check-off system (whereby union dues are deducted automatically from pay). The Industrial Council ruled that the NUTW was not represented sufficiently widely in the industry as a whole and the dispute between the unions will now be resolved in an industrial court.

Further evidence of TUCSA's incorporation in the Government's labour relations strategy has been graphically shown in a survey (published in early 1984) of the wage levels of artisans (skilled workers) over the last 10 years. The study shows that artisans, who were largely represented by TUCSA unions for the period under review, suffered a real wage decline in negotiations conducted in the industrial council system. Gordon Young, one of the researchers involved in the report commented that the results would have a "disastrous" impact on the credibility of the unions involved. "Unions should be negotiating agreements which protect their members at all times rather than agreeing to wage levels which suit employers. The fact that artisans' wages have gone down speaks for itself. These people have had unions to represent them in the Industrial Councils and yet they have got poorer", he said.

Another issue which threatens TUCSA is the sharp decline in support from international labour organisations in favour of the independents.

These developments are encouraging splits within TUCSA itself. In June 1982, two unions with a combined membership of 11,000 workers in the catering and distributive trade withdrew from TUCSA as a result of dissatisfaction with the Council's policies. The splinter unions were concerned with TUCSA's distancing itself from the wave of protests from the independent unions following the death in detention in February 1982 of the union organiser Dr Neil Aggett.

The crisis of credibility facing TUCSA deepened in 1983. In October at the union's annual conference a major dispute broke out between affiliates arguing over the Council's increasingly hardline posture against the independent and non-racial unions. TUCSA's leadership urged the government to increase action to prevent illegal strikes and to ban the unregistered unions.

In protest at the "selfish" and "imbecillic" attitude of the TUCSA leadership, the South African Boilermakers Society withdrew from the union soon after the annual conference. The 54,000 strong mixed race union, led by Ike Van der Watt, argues that TUCSA has lost credibility and its sense of direction. The failure to adapt the union at a time of rapid change in South Africa's labour relations scene has meant that TUCSA 'is unable to satisfy the needs of a large number of workers now able to join the union movement", says Van der Watt.

The Boilermakers departure further alienates TUCSA from the

organisations of the international trade union movement. As the largest South African affiliate of the International Metalworkers' Federation, the Boilermakers have strong international links and participates in the IMF's South Africa Coordinating Council along with unions affiliated to CUSA and FOSATU. Indeed, in March 1984, Van Der Watt was elected President of the Coordinating Council which brings together South Africa's ten largest metal unions, representing 200,000 workers. In 1984, a further eight unions withdrew from TUCSA.

FOSATU

The best organised of the independent union federations is the Federation of South African Trade Unions (FOSATU). It was established in 1979 and in November 1983 boasted a membership of 106,000 workers organised in approximately 490 factories. A further indication of FOSATU's increasing strength are the number of companies which recognise the federation's shop stewards and negotiating rights. To date FOSATU have obtained, or are negotiating, over 285 company recognition agreements.

At its bi-annual congress in April 1979, FOSATU adopted a programme of objectives which indicate the union's basic policy positions. FOSATU has attempted to achieve:

● a strong democratic factory floor organisation;
● a united labour movement, independent of race, colour, creed or sex;
● national industrial unions;
● an ongoing worker education programme;
● Social justice, decent standards of living and fair conditions of work for affiliates and for the working class as a whole.

(*Source:* Introduction to FOSATU Annual Report 1981).

FOSATU's nine affiliated unions are particularly strong in the heavy industrial sector, organising car workers, metal workers, food workers, transport workers, and textile workers among others. The membership is predominantly black although the union is committed to a non-racial policy.

FOSATU has assumed a key role in the emerging structure of the independent South African labour movement. The federation has continued to grow despite consistent state harassment. In 1980, for example, the South African government prohibited "the collection of contributions by or for or on behalf of Federation of South African Trade Unions (FOSATU)". The ban not only prevents FOSATU from obtaining funds inside South Africa, but seeks to block funds going to the Federation from the international labour movement, a development condemned by the International Confederation of Free Trade Unions (ICFTU) as "contrary to accepted international labour standards".

The FOSATU unions have also had to contend with the drive by the TUCSA 'parallel' union to recruit black workers. In response FOSATU has fiercely attacked the parallels as being organised in connivance with management, as condoning the state structure of racially exclusive unions, and of seriously assisting black workers only in the face of competition from the independent unions.

Following the legislation introduced as a result of the Wiehahn Commission, the FOSATU unions opted to apply for registration. FOSATU believes that advantages can be gained that would compensate for the controls that the government imposes on registered unions. They argued that company recognition would offer some protection from state repression, and provide unions the benefit of subscriptions checkoff. However, FOSATU has insisted on seeking registration on a non-racial basis. As a consequence of this commitment FOSATU unions have faced difficulties in registering. In 1980, for example, the FOSATU affiliated Metal and Allied Worker Union applied for registration stressing their wish to organise on a non-racial basis. The Government responded by providing MAWU with a registration certificate but only to represent African workers. The union rejected this offer and successfully appealed to the Natal Supreme Court which upheld MAWU's protest and thus overturned the tradition of racial registration.

Another controversial issue for FOSATU is the system of Industrial Councils which are at the centre of South Africa's labour relations structure. The Councils have traditionally been viewed as a device to separate negotiations from the shop floor favouring the interests of the minority of workers at the expense of the black majority. In addition the Council's lengthy disputes procedures inhibit the legal right to strike. FOSATU have campaigned to remove the existing Industrial Council system in favour of one catering for plant-level bargaining.

Meanwhile FOSATU, after a long internal debate, has allowed affiliates to join Industrial Councils if the unions wish and provided that plant based bargaining and recognition rights were not lost.

One dramatic aspect of the independent trade unions is the quality and range of black working class leadership it has produced. Chris Dlamini is senior shop steward at Kellogs in Springs and president of FOSATU. He is a natural leader as much at home in the corridors of an international conference as talking to a handful of shop stewards. He has always fought for workers' rights. "I remember once when the company introduced a canteen system, where you could get a quarter of a loaf of bread for free. The old lady who was running the canteen used to supply us with stale bread and people used to grumble but they never did anything. Well, one day I had had enough of this stale bread so I went back to her. Look, I said, the company decided to give us bread but it never said you should give us stale bread. She started swearing at me, so I threw the bread into a basket next to the counter. Well, she phoned the general manager who came in and dragged me by my dustcoat to the top manager's office. He told me I should be dismissed for such an action but I asked for a chance to defend myself. I stated my reasons why I rejected the bread and even brought the stale bread to him. Well, he said to me, don't you think you should have adopted a different attitude when you spoke to the white woman. I replied that I don't know. If one is angry it doesn't matter if the person is white or black as far as I am concerned. In spite of everybody expecting me to be fired, I wasn't," Dlamini recalls. He was elected to the liaison committee at Rank Xerox, where Dlamini worked before Kellogs, but said that the liaison committees were powerless to act for workers. "Workers would give us a mandate to make demands but when we arrived at the meeting it was dominated by management and some supervisors. Immediately the chairman, who is always one of the management, wants to close the matter, he just closes it. And if you are dissatisfied you are told that you can find a job somewhere else. At times we managed to air grievances and the bosses would say they would investigate the matter and come back to us — but nothing ever happened. Because of our powerlessness we were forced to talk about whether the forks and knives were nice, whether the lawn was OK or whether we had enough equipment for sports."

Dlamini said that before the arrival of the independent unions "what was really aggravating was that workers could be dismissed without any notice and for no apparent reason. And as a result of this dismissal, a worker would lose his house, children would be forced to leave school and that would mean a dead end for that family's future." He felt that the presence of the union at Kellogs certainly eliminated some of these malpractices as workers could elect representatives of their own choice who would fight for them. "The presence of the union means that a balance of power has emerged between management and the workers. If workers are well organised, the bosses are forced to realise that we are not just people who produce things in their factory but real human beings with rights. In Kellogs, through the union we have blocked retrenchments, we have fought for a living wage and in 1983 we achieved R2 an hour. Workers deserve a fair share of what they have produced and this can be achieved by a workers organisation. But it must be worker controlled and that is why FOSATU sees workers control as crucial for the building of an organisation which will help the working class," Dlamini declared.

In April 1982 FOSATU held a second Congress to review the achievements since the inauguration in 1979. The Congress was held at Hamanskrall, near Pretoria, and resulted in an important statement of FOSATU's policies and objectives. In an address to the Congress, FOSATU's General Secretary, Joe Foster, spoke of the need to build an independent workers movement which would ensure that workers "control their own destiny". Describing past popular struggles in South Africa, Foster explained that until now the creation of a workers' movement had been impossible. "Progressive and militant unions were continually the subject of state harassment . . . Whilst the unions were often prominent they were always small and weakly organised both nationally and in the factories". Foster believes that the environment today is different. Changes in the economy and in black workers' levels of skill and education allow the creation of a powerful workers' movement.

Under these conditions Foster says that FOSATU must concentrate on building factory floor support in the major industries. Although praising the role of the liberation movements and the African National Congress in particular, FOSATU will remain independent from any political organisations. FOSATU does not regard itself as apolitical, but rather that the establishment of a worker movement is in itself a political task. According to Joe Foster "workers must strive to build their own powerful and effective organisation even whilst they are part of a wider popular struggle" (see Appendix 1).

At the conclusion of the Hammanskral Congress a resolution was adopted calling for one-man-one-vote and deploring the bantustan policy "whereby South African citizens are stripped of their birthright and declared foreigners in the country of their birth". The resolution stated that FOSATU will engage in struggles "to secure a better standard of living, social justice, social security and the political emancipation of workers in the community where members of its affiliates live". FOSATU also added that "an essential prerequisite" for change is to develop at the factory level an "unshakeable unity based on effective organisation".

The emphasis on factory organisation, however, has not inhibited the Federation's involvement in wider issues. The union has engaged in a series of unity talks with the other emerging unions and has tackled the Government's constitutional proposals which extend certain democractic rights to Asians and coloureds, but not to blacks. FOSATU has clearly stated its opposition to the Government's reform plans arguing that they are 'undemocratic, racist and anti-worker''. To back up its protest FOSATU mounted a major educational programme among workers and a wider campaign against the Government's referendum held in November 1983.

FOSATU has not joined either of the two main organisations campaigning against the constitutional reforms, ie; the United Democratic Front and the National Forum Committee. Rather FOSATU has been concerned to maintain its distinct working class identity and simply express support for the aims of the two organisations whilst organising its own, union based, campaigns.

The FOSATU unions are usually affiliated to appropriate international Trade Secretariats and have engaged in highly effective international solidarity work.

CUSA

The second trade union centre of independent unions is the Council of South African Unions (CUSA). It was created in September 1980 after the failure of its unions to resolve differences with the FOSATU national centre.

The principle difference between the two is over the question of race in the short and medium term. Both unions share the goal of the creation in the long term of a non-racial labour movement. FOSATU believes that this can only come about by pursuing a non-racial policy from the outset.

CUSA is closer to what is commonly termed the 'black consciousness' philosophy which encourages a positive effort to construct an exclusively black leadership. Both federations are open to unions of all races, but CUSA's affiliates are only black unions.

CUSA consists of ten unions with approximately 148,000 members and is mainly based in the Transvaal area. Unlike FOSATU's tightly disciplined unions, CUSA is a loose federation which seeks only to co-ordinate affiliates on certain principal issues. CUSA has not advocated registration or non-registration to its affiliates. Rather it has pointed out the advantages and disadavantages of both actions. Currently two CUSA affiliates have been permitted to register.

CUSA has established strong links with the international labour movement, particularly via the International Confederation of Free Trade Unions (ICFTU), to which it is affiliated.

The most important of CUSA's affiliates is the National Union of Mineworkers (NUM) led by Secretary General Cyril Ramaphosa (who previously worked in CUSA's legal department). The NUM was created in 1982 and has already gained a membership of 70,000 of whom 70 per cent work in the gold mines and 25 per cent in coal mines. The union is recognised by 14 companies and is also recognised by the Chamber of Mines for negotiating purposes.

Despite the problems of organising the high percentage of migrant workers that are employed in the mining industry, the NUM has become an impressive force in the South African labour movement. The union demanded a 30 per cent wage rise in negotiations with the Chamber of Mines in 1983 and has fought hard to raise health and safety issues which are obviously crucial in the industry.

Other Unions

Apart from the two national federations, FOSATU and CUSA, described above, there are a group of significant independent, individual unions. These unions include the African Food and Canning Workers' Union, the Black Media Workers' Association, the General Workers' Union, the Black Municipal Workers' Union, the Motor Assemblies and Component Workers' Union and the South African Allied Workers' Union (SAAWU). From this group the most important are SAAWU and the Cape Town area unions — the General Workers' Union and the African Food and Canning Workers' Union.

SAAWU

The most overtly political of the independent trade unions is the South African Allied Workers' Union (SAAWU). Based in the East London area, SAAWU was established in March 1979 following a split in the black consciousness-inspired Black Allied Workers' Union. The breakaway group established SAAWU and committed the union to a policy of non racialism. The union's President, Thozamile Gqwetha, explains that "we believe the country has a non-racial future and therefore we must be totally non-racial."

SAAWU claims a membership of 50,000 and has been described as "as much a mass movement as a union", but one researcher suggests that a membership of 20,000 is a more realistic estimate. Committed to a policy of mass participatory democracy, SAAWU has sought to establish a strong relationship with the black community. A union spokesman explains that "SAAWU is a trade union dealing with workers who are part and parcel of the community. Transport, rents to be paid, are also worker issues. The problems of the workplace go outside the workplace".

As a result SAAWU has become heavily involved in political

issues beyond conventional factory disputes. SAAWU says that "there can be no normal unionism in an abnormal society". The union has challenged the South African's homelands policy and, in particular, opposed the so-called 'independence' of the Ciskei bantustan in which many of SAAWU's members live. The Ciskei gained 'independence' from South Africa in December 1981 and SAAWU's activities have seriously challenged its legitimacy.

In contrast to the FOSATU unions, SAAWU has totally rejected registration with the government and ignores the official bargaining system. SAAWU has stated that it will not register unless the basis of the apartheid system is removed; that is the abolition of such racial legislation as the pass laws and the Group Areas Act.

Despite SAAWU's militant posture, the union has been able to gain a number of company recognition agreements. Notable recognitions have been obtained from South African Chlorides, Johnson and Johnson, and KSM Milling. Such agreements were reached after representative elections showed that SAAWU had majority support on the shop floor. The personnel director of Chlorides, Theo Heffer, believes that "to refuse to deal with a representative union, even if it is not registered, would, to my mind, fly in the face of reality. We are concerned with representation not registration. If a union reflects the true representation of the workers, then one is courting disaster to refuse to deal with that union".

Such a liberal approach by management was notably absent in the South African subsidiary of Rowntrees-Mackintosh. In February 1981, 500 black workers and SAAWU members were sacked from the Wilson-Rowntree factory in East London after a strike over unfair dismissals. The management refused to recognise SAAWU and maintains its long-standing relationship with the docile TUCSA affiliated Sweet Workers' Union. SAAWU have responded by launching a boycott of Wilson-Rowntrees products. Leaflets printed with the slogan 'Spit out that fruit gum chum' were circulated by Boycott Support Committees causing an estimated 25 per cent loss of business for the company. However, more than any other independent union SAAWU has been subject to severe state harassment. The union's participatory and community orientated political stand has antagonised the South African government and the authorities of the Ciskei. Scores of SAAWU members were detained by the Ciskei police in 1981 and the South Africans have assisted the homeland administration in union busting techniques. Leaders of SAAWU have been subject to long periods of detention during which at least one of them had to have hospital treatment.

Thozamile Gqweta, SAAWU's 30 year old president, has been

described as South Africa's most harassed black trade union leader. Since the founding of SAAWU Gqweta has been detained nine times and was held in the notorious John Vorster Square prison where Neil Aggett died. During his fifth period of detention, in February 1982, Gqweta was transferred to the psychiatric ward of Johannesburg hospital. After a visit by relatives it was reported that he was suffering from a severe headache, depression and anxiety, difficulty in speaking, partial memory loss, as well as a dramatic loss in weight.

In March 1981 Gqweta narrowly escaped assassination when his house was destroyed by arsonists. He survived by climbing through a window as the door had been wired up to prevent his escape. In November the same year, his mother and uncle were burnt to death when their house was similarly burnt down. At their funeral a few days later there were clashes between the Ciskei homeland police and the 3,000 mourners. During the violence, Gqweta's 20 year old girlfriend Deliswa Roxiso was shot dead.

In December 1981, Thozamile Gqweta as asked if he was afraid of the police repression. He replied: "Police tactics are to make you scared, but they won't succeed. If anything they have made me more determined. But these latest incidents have changed me. I used to laugh a lot. Now there is great anger inside me".

The onslaught against Gqweta and SAAWU represent an attempt by the South African and Ciskei authorities to destry the union. SAAWU has been adamantly opposed to the 'independence' of the Ciskei, granted by South Africa in December 1981. The Ciskei's 'President', Lennox Sebe, is committed to crushing SAAWU in the belief that independent unions are unnecessary since the "Ciskei itself is a trade union looking after workers' intersts".

The bantustan's security police, the Ciskei Central Intelligence Service (CCIS) were responsible for the largest mass arrest of trade unionists when they detained some 200 peole after a meeting at Mdantsane in East London in October 1982. The workers were accused of having sung freedom songs and anti-Ciskei government slogans. They were detained for ten days before being charged with violations under the Riotous Assemblies Act.

Co-operation in union busting between Ciskei and the South African security has been explicit. A document written by an officer in the Security Branch of the South African Police on how to break the power of SAAWU was circulated to companies in the area. It proposed the encouragement of TUCSA unions and in the creation of lists of unemployed workers to be used to recruit labour for replacing dismissed SAAWU members. In October 1980, the Minister of Manpower Fanie Botha held a meeting behind closed doors with East London employers urging them to hold out against SAAWU. Equally the Ciskei police have publicly acknowledged their relationship with the South Africans.

The problem facing SAAWU is whether it can retain its militant posture, and inevitably endure further repression, without losing its membership. Resistance by employers also weakens SAAWU's support since repeated strike action defeated by scab labour leaves many of the union's members unemployed. To try to counteract this trend SAAWU established an unemployed workers branch, but met with little success.

Adding to SAAWU's difficulties is a major split in the union's leadership which occured in early 1984. Three senior officials including the General Secretary Sam Kikine were expelled from the union. Announcing the expulsions SAAWU's President Thozamile Gqweta refused to provide reasons for the action but it appears that personality tensions within the leadership are primarily responsible. Kikine is based in Durban whilst Gqweta and the new General Secretary Sisa Njikelana operate from East London. The rival leaders have adopted markedly different styles of organisation with Gqweta being credited with a more professional approach to unionism.

It remains to be seen if the split generates a major change of policy within SAAWU, particularly over the issue of trade union unity. As yet SAAWU has been reluctant to shed its 'community-union' image and fully co-operate with the unity talks being held by the other major independent unions. Following the expulsions Gqweta reiterated SAAWU's traditional policy approach and it appears the union will maintain it cautious attitude to the unity moves.

Cape Unions

The Cape Unions share a common commitment rather than a formal organisation. The African Food and Canning Workers' Union and the F & CWU were two of the few unions to survive the repression of the 1960's. Both were affiliates of the exiled South African Congress of Trade Unions (SACTU). The General Workers Union was founded in 1978 as the Western Province General Workers Union, which in turn, owes its birth to a workers' advice centre set up in 1973. The three unions share a commitment to non-racialism but have a predominantly African membership. The General Workers Union established itself as a 'general' union rather than an industrial union due to the small percentage of Africans in the workforce of the area. In Cape Town, the state designated the region as a 'Coloured Preference Area' which requires employers to hire Africans only when no 'coloureds' are available. As a result the coloured workers dominate the skilled job sector with Africans concentrated in the low paid and unskilled jobs.

The General Workers Union's 12,000 members cover most of the stevedores employed in South Africa's four major ports and it is steadily increasing its recruitment of engineering industry workers. To find the GWU's national chairman you have to drive due west of Cape Town through the coloured areas, skirt the notorious African shanty town Crossroads township until you come to a men's hostel at Nyango East. The room in which Johnson Mpukumpa, a migrant worker who works in a small metal factory, lives is about 4 metres by 3 metres. He has shared it for sixteen years with another migrant worker. He sees his wife and four children who live in Transkei at Easter and Christmas and sends most of the R80 a week he earns to them.

"Every worker would like to stay with his family, but many cannot. So it is the duty of the union to take up issues like influx control,'' said Mpukumpa. The general secretary of the GWU, David Lewis, is white. Says Mpukumpa, "If we say we are democratic we can allow no hint of racism. Colour is not the question. The question is whether a union represents its members or not.'' The relationship of white union organisers with black workers is discussed elsewhere. For Mpukumpa it is a question of developing leadership from within the working class and not relying passively on key union figures. "Workers join the union to have a channel to express their grievances. Without the union the workers are voiceless. But the union must be run by the workers themselves. They must take the decisions. It is not good for a leader to run alone and leave the workers behind. Workers and leaders must all grow up together,'' he stated.

CCAWUSA

The Commercial Catering and Allied Workers Union of South Africa is a driving force in the food and retail industry. Originally aligned with CUSA it is now unaffiliated. In 1984 it had a membership of 40,000 and has won recognition agreements with several important employers. It has also participated in the unity talks to try and bring FOSATU, CUSA and unaffiliated unions into one federation.

Chapter 4

Sheltering the Flame: the Growth of Unions after 1973

The bold steps taken by black workers in the 'Durban' strikes of 1973 may, in retrospect, seem to have been destined to succeed. At the time that was certainly not the view. Many thought that they were more likely to fail. Not only did the strike wave gradually subside, reaching a low point in 1977 when strikes were only a quarter of the level that they reached in 1973, but the union movement had been hit by two attacks from the state. In 1974 and 1976 trade union organisers in key unions were banned and prevented from taking any further part in the union movement for the next five years. Some felt so helpless in the wake of their being banned that they left the country, determined to continue the struggle from exile, much in the way in which SACTU militants had done in the 1960s.

As Steve Friedman, the labour correspondent of the *Rand Daily Mail*, the country's most liberal newspaper, and one of the most respected labour analysts was to write later: "The initial wave of organisation was to prove as ephemeral as its predecessors. The banning of union leaders — all white intellectuals — began a decline which was to see paid-up union membership in the Durban area slump to something in the region of 2,000 by the mid-1970s. In retrospect, it seemed that the brief wave of unionism in the early Seventies was to be yet another chapter in the catalogue of the African union movement's failures."

But this pessimistic prognosis proved mistaken. The unions have succeeded, they have grown, and they have become a powerful force on the South African political scene. There are distinct, but interrelated, reasons for their success.

1. *Who joined the unions?*

The first reason for the union's success has been the courage and determination of black workers. But, having said that, it is important not to fetishise this, for the eternally optimistic, all-seeing worker militant is a myth. In reality, workers are as much prone to depression and despair as any other class. The question that needs to be answered is which workers joined the unions, and which workers refused. The answer is by no means clear, but one study conducted in Durban towards the end of 1975 gives some clues. The survey was conducted amongst the membership of the three most powerful unions in the Durban area — the Chemical Workers Industrial Union, the Metal and Allied Workers Union and the National Union of Textile Workers. All were, in time, to become members of FOSATU. At that time they had between them just under 14,000 workers signed up, but the real strength of their base is revealed from the number that were paid up members: CWIU — 900, MAWU — 1,000, NUTW — 2,000. Between them the unions had 14 paid officials some of whom were part-time.

The majority of workers that joined the unions could be described in the following terms. They were unskilled or had low grade, semi-skilled employment They were young — most were under 50, and over half were under 40. Nearly three-quarters had been in their current employment for over two years, and 5 per cent had been in their jobs over 15 years. Just over half had been born in the rural areas, and a third were born in Durban. For the vast majority their union was the first that they had joined, but a significant number (11 per cent) had been members of SACTU in the 1960s — a factor that explained the continued popularity of Moses Mabheda, a SACTU leader of the 60s, who was mentioned by 8 per cent of the union members, when asked which leader could best improve their lot.

Arbitrary management action and victimisation was put as equally important as low wages by the workers, and nearly 60 per cent of the workers put defending workers rights as the most important reason for joining a union. But when asked whether the union was helping to overcome their problems less than half (49 per cent) were able to answer in the affirmative. 45 per cent felt that the union's performance could not be judged because it was not recognised and its members were too vulnerable to victimisation. As one worker put it: "This is very difficult because most of the things need an open challenge, yet we can't do it because we can then be exposing ourselves to victimisation by police and management." Not surprisingly fear of victimisation was seen as the most important issue dissuading workers from joining unions, with pessimism put as the second most potent factor.

The academics who conducted the survey concluded: "We have shown that members in this sample are relatively stable in their jobs and join unions to try collectively to improve their wages and work conditions. These are the necessary conditions; the sufficient conditions for effective trade unions involve the readiness of both management and the state to allow the emergence of collective organisation in the work-place and a willingness to recognise and negotiate with its leadership on a permanent basis."

2. *Economic contradictions and the role of management*

Like the economies of most other capitalist states, the South African economy has in the past two decades witnessed increasing monopolisation. As South Africa followed other countries down the monetarist paths of the 1980s the rate of concentration increased. One company, the Anglo-American Corporation, holds 50 per cent of all the shares listed on the Johannesburg stock exchange. According to the *Financial Mail*, the South African business and finance weekly, five general corporations and three insurance companies now control the bulk of South Africa's private-sector infrastructure. Apart from the mining industry — gold and coal — the big corporations now exercise effective control over, amongst others, the food sector, alcohol, tobacco, packaging, chemicals, insurance, motors and the Press.

The public sector controls 58 per cent of South Africa's fixed capital stock and contributes 26 per cent to the country's GDP. One in three workers in South Africa is a state employee. The South African Iron and Steel Industrial Corporation (ISCOR), the Industrial Development Corporation (IDC), the Electricity Supply Commission (ESCOM), the Armaments Development and Production Corporation (ARMSCOR) and the South African Coal, Oil and Gas Corporation (SASOL) are among the major 'parastatal' companies which are effectively government controlled.

Gold is the major South African export and its price rose rapidly after President Nixon took the United States off the gold standard in 1971 (in 1971, the price of gold was US$35 per ounce; in 1984 it is US$380 an ounce, with surges up to $800 an ounce in between). In 1980 net gold output exceeded the value of all other exports combined. Coal exports are also increasing in importance. Between 1973 and 1980, coal production more than doubled and a quarter of the coal produced is exported, which makes coal South Africa's second biggest source of foreign exchange earnings after gold. Overall, South Africa is an exporter of raw materials and agricultural produce and an importer of manufactured goods. Nonetheless, despite low productivity, the South African manufacturing economy is relatively advanced and corresponds more to that of an advanced industrialised state, not dissimilar in profile to that of Australia, rather than a developing or newly industrialised economy. Low wages combined with the ability of the monopolies to set prices relatively free of market price competition pressure has helped ensure high profit levels: in 1982, South African firms earned profits of 24.8 per cent, compared with 6.5 per cent in the United Kingdom, 4.1 per cent in West Germany and 5.9 per cent in Switzerland.

Despite its cushion of gold and other exports South Africa has not escaped the effects of the world recession. Since 1981 there has been a fall of 4.2 per cent in Gross Domestic Product and manufacturing output in 1983 was down 9.1 per cent from 1981.

Inflation in 1983 was 11 per cent. Market Research Africa estimates that average household income for Africans rose less than 10 per cent in 1983, while the incomes of other population groups generally kept pace with inflation.

Although African workers in certain sectors, notably manufacturing, have achieved money wage increases in the past decade, these have generally only just kept pace with inflation.

Average money earnings of Africans as a percentage of those of whites, 1972 and 1982

Sector	1972	1982
Mining	5.47	17.79
Manufacturing	17.12	31.60
Electricity	21.72	26.76
Construction	16.05	18.35
Trade	21.72	24.94
Transport and communications	16.61	25.96

In May 1984, the *Financial Mail* noted: "Monopolies, ologopolies and cartels have become entrenched features of South Africa's economic life". Yet it is in just these sectors that the black unions have made the most substantial gains since 1973.

This is not accidental. During the 1973 strikes management had found itself at factory after factory facing a workforce that had simply walked off the job. Time and again managers found themselves faced with an angry crowd of workers who refused to elect leaders or engage in any kind of dialogue. As one worker insisted: "We don't need a committee. We need R30.00 a week". The reason for this reluctance to elect a leadership was clear — fear of victimisation by management or the police. But as the manager of Coronation Brick Co., the company at which the strikes began, said, he was neither willing nor able "to negotiate with 1,500 workers on a football field". It was a dilemma that management was to come across time and again during the dispute. And for the more thoughtful managers it held a clear message — if you want to be able to conduct reasonable negotiations with workers in the future, you had better come to terms with the leaders that they throw up from the factory floor. Simple repression is not going to solve the problem. And one of the results of the increasing monopolisation outlined above, was that these considerations spread rapidly through major sectors of the economy. Senior management realised that it could not achieve its goals of increased profits and a larger market share if it allowed local managers to simply remove any leader that stepped forward from amongst the workforce. This sophisticated analysis did not come easily, but it was assisted by two factors — the intense shortage of skilled labour and the international context within which many firms operated.

The shortage of skilled labour was probably the more important factor. According to a 1981 survey, the South African private sector had a skill shortage of 8 per cent in terms of craftsmen and apprentices and 12.1 per cent in terms of scientists, engineers and technicians. In 1982 there were 5,517 white apprentices under training in the metal engineering and 390 Africans. There were 807 coloured and 426 Asian apprentices in the same year. Although this was still not enough to provide the skills required by industry, it was a considerable advance from the situation in 1979, when no African apprentices were under training. With the white population static the employers had no alternative but to begin to train blacks for skilled positions.

Management was clearly aware of this problem. In a private study commissioned for the major multinationals and published in 1980, Business International pointed to the serious bottlenecks that had emerged in the economy as a result of the shortage of skilled labour, and concluded that the only solution was for management to train black workers to fill the places previously occupied by whites. They quoted with approval the progress made by the German firm Siemens. The Siemens chief executive, Wilfried Wentges said: "In 1966, we had only 10 blacks in skilled and semi-skilled wage-earning jobs. Now the number is 1,391, a most impressive result of untiring training. In 1966, only 2.4 per cent of our African wage earners could be classified as skilled or semi-skilled, but now the proportion is 26 per cent". Clearly no rational manager would be prepared to throw away the results of this 'untiring training', and this gave black workers a bargaining strength that they had previously lacked.

The international investment in the South African economy is central to the country's development. According to the Business International survey cited above, there are between 2,000 and 2,500 foreign owned firms operating in South Africa. By far and away the largest number are British (1,200) followed by German (350) and US (340) concerns. Total foreign investment is in the region of $30 billion. About 20 per cent of all industry in South Africa is accounted for by foreign investment.

Countries such as Japan are increasing their involvement but are doing so, for example in the auto industry, by setting up wholly owned South African firms so that the fiction of non-Japanese involvement in the apartheid system is maintained. In fact South Africa exports more to Japan (15.6 per cent) than to either the United States (12.3 per cent) or Great Britain (13.7 per cent). Taiwan has become an important export market, overtaking Canada in 1982. European and American firms have been there for a long time. Swedish companies such as SKF, Alfa Laval and Electrolux established subsidiaries in South Africa in the 1920s. Many British companies go back still further.

But the crucial point is that international companies are susceptible to international pressure in a way in which local companies are not. The Business International report recognised this point: "World antagonism to apartheid has increased in the last 20 years, although the growth in pressure against South Africa has been slow and steady rather than dramatic. The most significant development in the late 1970s has been the imposition by certain Western countries of economic embargoes to back up what has until now been largely a rhetorical campaign . . . Multi-nationals, by taking affirmative action to improve the working conditions of black employees, may be able to retard the introduction of stricter measures against South Africa and indeed against themselves."

So although the campaign for sanctions against South Africa may have failed to achieve its ultimate objective, namely economic sanctions, it has helped to create a climate in which international companies are aware of the spotlight that is focussed upon their activities. It was not accidental that the first company to recognise a black union in the 1970s was Smith and Nephew — a British subsidiary.

3. *Unions and the state: confusion, concessions and confrontations*

Discussing the South African state is never easy, for it takes so many forms. At the one level there is the South African Parliament, which, until September 1984, operated under the Westminster model. With one grave exception — it only represented whites, for only they had the vote. But its flawed nature was further undermined by the fact that there is in reality no serious opposition. In September 1984 a new constitution gave coloureds and Asians representation in segregated Houses of Parliament, but whites still have the whip hand in governing the country. Since 1948 there has only been one party in power — the Nationalist Party. Since the government operates without an opposition it must respond to the pressures upon it as if it was the opposition itself, for there is no prospect of a future government of a different political complexion undoing the legislation that it enacts. Thus the laws that it brings in are quite frequently withdrawn or amended as a result of pressure from outside Parliament. The abandonment of legislation on pensions (described below), after an outcry from the black unions and a wave of strikes, is a case in point. But this is a somewhat isolated example. The more normal course of events is for the executive arm of the state to alter the law administratively without formally going through the motions of having the law amended. So one often finds that a particular piece of legislation is simply no longer enforced. But, since the law still stands, most trade unionists in South Africa go about their business from day to day knowing that what they do more often than not contravenes some law, but hoping that the law will not be enforced. The degree of enforcement often varies widely from area to area, so that something that might be generally accepted in Cape Town or Johannesburg, would result in instant arrest in any small town in the Orange Free State — the heart of Afrikanerdom.

The state is further complicated by the bantustans — which are today referred to as 'homelands'. For although they are regarded by most of the world as part of South Africa and under the South African state, they are seen as independent by Pretoria. And some of the most fearsome repression meted out to trade unionists has come from the bantustans. The Ciskei, in particular, has become notorious for its overt hostility to any form of unionisation.

But despite these obstacles, it is difficult to discern a clear strategy that the state has attempted to employ in South Africa. The most obvious has been repression, and no-one should be under any illusion about the dangers under which the unions operate in the country. Union leaders and activists have been banned, jailed and even killed. And as the following table indicates, this is a trend that has not diminished over time.

Number of occasions police called:

	1974	1980	1983
a. to a labour dispute	38	52	65
b. to a work stoppage	14	20	22
c. to a strike	51	94	99
Number of black workers arrested for striking illegally	214	294	525

To this chilling list could be added the death in detention of the trade union official, Neil Aggett in early 1982, and the detention and harassment of Thozamile Gqweta, the President of the South African Allied Workers Union. Not only were his mother and uncle burnt to death when the door of his house was wired shut, and the place then set ablaze, but his girl friend was shot and he was taken into prison and so brutally treated that he became severely depressed and lost his memory.

But if this was the only response that the state had found to the unions they would, in all likelihood, have ceased to exist. In the wake of the 1973 strikes the state embarked upon an alternative approach. This change in emphasis was signalled by the introduction of the Bantu Labour Relations Regulations Amendment Act of 1973. The Act established two types of in-factory committees which were meant to be available as means of communication between black workers and white management. The committees — 'works' and 'liaison' committees — were a deliberate attempt to forestall the development of trade unions, and were denounced as such.

They were generally passive instruments of management, and workers became dissatisfied with this poor substitute for genuine representation. Nonetheless, they did provide workers with the first taste of bargaining — a novel experience for many. By 1979 there were 312 works committees and 2,683 liaison committees in operation.

But a far more significant step was taken with the appointment in 1977 of a Commission of Inquiry into Labour Legislation led by Nicholaas Wiehahn. The Commission, which was set up in the wake of the 1976 Soweto uprising, reflected the government's concern that the union movement was consolidating its position, and that it was doing so entirely outside the parameters of government control. In particular the government was worried about the politicisation of industrial relations as the 'class of '76' (young blacks politicised by the Soweto uprising) began to enter the workforce.

In what was described by Steve Friedman as "a bizarre piece of symbolism" the Wiehahn Commission released its report on May Day 1979. The Commission recommended a number of measures, but perhaps the most important was the recognition that blacks could form their own unions. Although such unions had not been illegal, they now received official recognition. This change ended 60 years of government policy aimed at forcing black unions out of existence, and driving all Africans into the bantustans.

In addition to this central proposal (which was accepted by the government) there were a number of other steps that the Commission recommended. These included the establishment of a new industrial court which was to attempt to resolve labour disputes, and a National Manpower Commission that was to provide surveillance over union activities. But the fundamental strategy was one of control. The Commission hoped to bring the black unions under the official industrial relations system that had previously only been available to white unions. These were the Industrial Councils. These Councils govern the terms and conditions of particular industries, setting wages, hours and standards of employment. Previously only white or coloured and Asian union members were represented directly on the Industrial Councils. African unions — or those offering membership to all groups — were prevented from registering with the Councils, and thus securing a place at the negotiations. Instead government officials had been appointed to act on behalf of Africans — with the predictable result that African wages were only a fraction of those paid to whites.

Now for the first time Africans would be allowed a place at the Industrial Council sessions. But only if they registered. This was something that the black unions rejected. For they saw the Industrial Councils as being remote from the real struggles that were taking place on the shop floor, and an attempt to remove the negotiations from the factories in which the unions had their real strength. The unions were as yet not strong enough to cope with negotiations on a national level.

For although some of the unions were beginning to pick up strength in particular industries in certain areas, none were strong enough to feel really representative at a national level. In addition some union officials felt that any form of registration was undesirable, since it involved contact with the apartheid state, which they believed would eventually bring them under state control.

These fears were expressed at the first union unity conference, held in Cape Town in August 1981. A statement adopted at that meeting stated: "Industrial Councils: the meeting rejected the present Industrial Council system as an acceptable means of collective bargaining. The meeting recommended that unions that are not members of Industrial Councils should not enter any Industrial Council and requested that participating unions refer this back to their respective unions for endorsement. The unions agreed to support each other in the event of any union resisting participation in the Industrial Council." The issue of Industrial Councils was to be a major bone of contention between the black unions as time went by, for as the resolution implied, some were already members of the Councils, and as the unions felt their strength grow, some began to believe that their best interests lay in having a presence at a national level, without giving up their commitment to shop-floor bargaining.

This position was adopted by the Metal and Allied Workers Union in 1983. The decision was defended by Andrew Zulu, then president of MAWU in an interview:

"Question: What prompted MAWU to apply for membership? (of the Industrial Council).

"Answer: During the 1981 and 1982 strikes on the East Rand we were negotiating with individual companies only and so while we won increases in some companies, employers were able to crush strikes in others. If we had been able to negotiate nationally, we could have at least won something everywhere — perhaps R2 an hour. Also we expanded after the strikes and are now organising in over 200 factories. We do not have time to have lengthy negotiations at each plant. Negotiations take six to twelve months. It would be easier to face employers nationally — and the only forum is the Industrial Council."

Other unions rejected this approach entirely, arguing that all the unions should follow the line agreed at Cape Town, and that to have any truck with the Councils was to arrive at an accommodation with the apartheid state. In practice both approaches have been followed, with varying degrees of success.

Strikes

If the response of the unions to the Wiehahn proposals was at best cool, the response from management was just the opposite. Many managers saw the Commission's recommendations as official endorsement of black unions, and the number of recognition agreements that were entered into by companies after Wiehahn snowballed. This process was accelerated by a rise in confidence on the part of workers, and a spate of bitter, but generally successful strikes that won nationwide coverage in the press. A strike at one of South Africa's best known food firms, Fattis and Monis, in their pasta factory in Cape Town in April 1979 was won after workers held out for seven months. After a community-wide boycott of the companies' products, and substantial sums of money had been donated by the public, the strikers won, and the union was recognised by the company. Hot on the heels of the settlement came a strike amongst stevedores on the Cape Town docks, and after a few days the employers there also gave in, and the docks were unionised. Not that the workers did not suffer reverses. A strike by meat workers collapsed, despite a four-month-long community boycott of all meat products. But the strike brought such a wave of bad publicity for the employers that many managers began to feel that it was not worth the poor image that was now associated with disregarding the unions.

As the following table indicates the confidence and combativity of black workers soared after the low that it had reached in 1977.

Strikes by black workers 1973-1983

Year	No. of Disputes	Black Workers on Strike
1973	370	98,029
1974	384	58,975
1975	276	23,295
1976	248	26,931
1977	90	15,091
1978	106	14,088
1979	101	17,323
1980	207	56,286
1981	342	84,705
1982	394	141,517
1983	336	64,469

In their fight for elementary rights and better wages it has been this upsurge of militancy that has not only won workers a better deal, but led to the phenomenal growth in the strength of the unions. It should not be forgotten that when it was formed in 1979 FOSATU had only 35,000 members, many of whom were not paid up. Today FOSATU has over 106,000 members.

In 1982, FOSATU affiliated unions were involved in 145 strikes with 90,000 workers taking part. This compares with CUSA where 10,000 workers took part in 13 strikes or SAAWU which organised 6 strikes involving 2,600 workers.

Yet the use of the strike weapon in South Africa has to be handled with care. For a start, most strikes are illegal; in fact there has been only one legal strike by a black union since 1981. To go on strike legally requires that a union first goes through a lengthy procedure designed to wear down union determination and to try and put as much time between the cause of the dispute and any industrial action undertaken to resolve it.

Once on strike, unions have to face further problems. Picketing is forbidden, though some unions have been gingerly organising poster campaigns outside strike-hit workplaces. Strike pay is illegal. Under both the Internal Security Act and the Riotous Assembly Act the police can arrest strikers or unions' officials for organising workers' meetings. Companies are legally entitled to dismiss workers during a strike. Inter-union rivalry has led to management successfully using others unions to help break strikes. During the Johannesburg municipal workers' strike, white citizens undertook what to them was the remarkable and unprecedented labour of rubbish disposal in order to undermine the strikers.

Why do workers go on strike? A breakdown of the reasons for strikes in 1982 in three key industrial sectors is shown in the table on the following page.

Most strikes are of short duration. In the auto industry in 1982 the average length was 5 days and in the metal industry 2½ days. Some last longer. In September 1982, 260 workers at the B&S Engineering factory in Brits (Transvaal) were dismissed after lodging a pay demand. The company tried to hire back workers selectively but this was rejected. The workers met every day in a church hall. The dispute lasted just over a year. Their union, MAWU, took the company to court accusing it of unfair labour practices and claimed R850,000 in back pay, the biggest such claim ever made. Finally, the company gave way and in September 1983 re-hired all the workers and agreed to establish a 'satisfactory' relationship with the union.

Often companies refuse to recognise unions and when a strike takes place insist that they will only talk to the workers directly and not to an 'outside party', i.e. the union. In May 1983, Progress Knitting in Natal, dismissed two workers for alleged low production and then, following a short protest stoppage by 28 of the sacked workers' colleagues, they fired another six for being 'trouble-makers'. This led, in turn, to a strike by the 1,500-strong workforce. Officials of the workers' union, the National Union of Textile Workers, offered to negotiate with the management who replied that they would talk only with the workers. The strikers refused, insisting the union represent them. Management attempts to split the workers by dismissing some of them failed as all those on strike refused *en bloc* to accept their wages. The strike dragged on for seven days until finally the Department of Manpower intervened; government officials produced a face-saving formula which allowed the company to go back on its previous position and agree to meet the union. Following this the union was fully recognised at Progress and shop stewards were elected.

In May 1981 a dispute occurred between the FOSATU affiliated Chemical Workers Industrial Union (CWIU) and the management of a Colgate-Palmolive plant in Boksburg.

The dispute, which lasted about 14 months, began over a recognition agreement. Colgate-Palmolive refused to recognise the CWIU on the grounds that it was unregistered, despite the fact that the union had the support of the majority of the workforce. Eventually Colgate gave in to the CWIU's demand for recognition but on condition that the union should negotiate on wages and conditions at an Industrial Council.

Main Strike Demands, 1982

DEMANDS

INDUSTRIAL SECTOR		Wages	Recognition	Dismissal	Retrench-ments	Pension Funds	Other	Unknown
Metal	1	36	3	10	11	3	4	2
	2	12,654	1,590	3,210	4,900	3,100	479	500
Motor	1	14		8	4		1	
	2	28,000		12,489	12,100		700	
Mines	1	13						
	2	70,500						

1. Represents the number of strikes in each sector.
2. Represents the number of strikers in each sector.

Without hesitation the CWIU refused to accept this condition and launched a two-pronged attack on the company. Firstly the union launched a consumer boycott of Colgate products and then began the process to declare a 'legal' strike. The CWIU had to apply to a Conciliation Board which found it could not resolve the dispute. After the Board, the union had to observe a 30-day 'cooling-off' period after which a strike could be legally declared if a ballot of the workers agreed — which they did, voting 93 per cent in favour of a strike.

Meanwhile the FOSATU-organised boycott of Colgate products gained momentum. Within two weeks thousands of workers were going to work with boycott stickers on their overalls and posters supporting the CWIU appeared in workers hostels. Traders in East Rand and elsewhere agreed to remove Colgate products from their shelves and whole communities became mobilised behind the boycott call. Other employers began to fear that a wave of sympathy strikes would occur. "What is clear", remarked the *Rand Daily Mail*, "is that workers in other East Rand factories as well as black community organisations were rallying behind the boycott".

Under such extreme pressure and just two days before the strike was due Colgate-Palmolive relented and agreed to negotiate with the CWIU outside of the Industrial Council. Colgate said that it had to "recognise the reality of the situation", and FOSATU hailed the settlement as an important victory. In its Annual Report FOSATU commented that "the Colgate-Palmolive dispute was a turning point in South Africa's industrial relations. It punched a great hole in the collective solidarity of employers . . .". The dispute also clearly indicated the power of boycott actions. "It was", says FOSATU, "a planned boycott and not one organised after a defeat had already taken place".

Proposed state legislation designed to control company pension schemes may appear an unlikely candidate for a major cause of strikes, yet in 1981 the government proposals sparked off a wave of strikes that rippled on into 1982. At the height of the controversy a total of 62 strikes occurred relating to the Pensions Bill in Natal alone, and by the end of 1981 the government had been forced to drop the Bill altogether.

The state had proposed to introduce the 'Preservation of Pensions Bill'. This seemingly innocuous legislation was to have ensured that companies continued to administer the pensions of their employees after they had left their employment — effectively locking in the pensions until the workers retired at 65.

Black workers' hostility to the proposal arose from a very real fear that once they left a company they would never see their contributions again. Given workers' experience of the almost insuperable difficulties of claiming money from the government's unemployment insurance fund (to which they also contribute) this is hardly surprising. There was also a belief that by 'preserving' pensions the state would shed its obligation to pay even the below subsistence pension that it pays at present to black workers.

Most of all there was the fact that most workers see their pension contributions as a form of savings to be used when they lose their jobs. It is about the only form of security that they possess. Certainly black workers were incensed that the state should be tampering with their finances without even bothering to consult them.

The Pension Gap: Monthly pensions 1980

White	Coloured and Asian	African
R109 (£55)	R62 (£32)	R33 (17)

Their response was not only to strike, but to demand the immediate payout of their contributions. Company after company was forced to comply, with a devastating effect on finances, which had relied in part on the pensions to fund company operations. Transvaal clothing workers alone were reported to have withdrawn over £500,000 of their pension contributions.

Management suggested that the whole matter was a 'misunderstanding' and said that if only the Bill was explained to workers it would be accepted. This was refuted by a FOSATU spokesman, saying "They understand the Bill . . . and they don't accept it. Workers have got pretty good reasons for not liking the Bill". Such was the opposition that on 6 November 1981 the Director General of Manpower was forced to announce that the Bill was to be withdrawn for consultation, and thereafter it was abandoned.

Despite the government climb-down, workers' interest in the control of their pensions has been awakened, and the first six months of 1982 saw a further 27 strikes on this issue in Natal. In July this came to a head with 3,000 workers on strike in Richards Bay. Workers are simply no longer willing to allow companies to use their money for whatever they like, and are demanding a say in its allocation. A FOSATU organiser said "Pension fund trustees, who have negotiated on several issues, seem to be missing the main point — that is that the people here in Natal don't seem to want a pension fund. They would rather have the money now and use it for the education of their children".

The industrial court

Another element in the Wiehahn proposals has proved to be a surprisingly effective weapon in the union's arsenal — the Industrial Court. Many unions now find the Court a useful adjunct to their industrial muscle. A number of recognition agreements have been forced upon companies and workers' confidence has been enhanced by the knowledge that wholesale sackings are made more difficult by the rulings of the Court. Not that the Court has made unions less combative. FOSATU unions have been in the forefront of the movement to use the Court in certain circumstances, and yet according to a recent survey FOSATU unions were involved in more strikes in 1983 than all other unions combined.

Just how the state will finally relate to the growing challenge that the union movement represents remains to be seen. Already there are signs that the power of the Industrial Court is to be curbed, and there are reports that the government intends to bring in new legislation to try to force all unions to register. But the gains of the last decade will not be easy to wipe away, and the power of the black unions looks like remaining a permanent factor in the South African political economy.

Chapter 5

Organisation and Structure

John Gomomo is the burly chairman of the shop steward's committee at the Volkswagen factory in Uitenhage, near Port Elizabeth. As he walks quickly down the lines where the Golf motor cars are assembled, most of the workers look up and grin. He stops for a word with some of them. The union notice board is covered with announcements and appeals from his union, the National Automobile and Allied Workers Union — NAAWU. He proudly points to three little offices that the company was building for shop stewards inside the plant. Outside, workers come up to discuss minor personal problems. Gomomo led two major strikes which hit Volkswagen in 1980 and 1982. Although the union had already been recognised by Volkswagen, an important advance after those strikes was the recognition of full-time shop stewards. Gomo also serves on NAAWU's executive council and is a member of FOSATU's National Executive. He is a type of trade union activist recognisable all over the world, sitting on a myriad of committees and taking decisions in which information gained through daily shop floor contacts informs his attitude when deciding upon a national FOSATU issue, just as his participation in national union leadership helps when deciding what strategy and tactics to adopt in plant level relations with Volkswagen management.

Unions' structures are affected by their sense of history and the relationship the workers feel they have with each other, with the employer and the state. South Africa is no different. The re-birth of South Africa trade unionism for black workers after 1973 was based firmly on democratic control by the membership and the establishment of strong workplace organisation. This was partly in reaction against the white-controlled trade unions with their emphasis on professional trade union officials working in close proximity with employers in the industrial councils. Perhaps even more important was the memory of how the previous waves of black trade unionisation had been more like general mass movements of workers, without strong roots in the workplace. The older generation of trade union activists shared with the young white intellectuals, who staffed worker advice centres in the early 1970s, the view that organisation in the factory or the warehouse should be central. Instead of going once every few months to hear a charismatic union leader deliver a rousing oration at a mass meeting, workers would elect local leaders and collectively discuss their problems. Employers too would have to confront and learn to negotiate with representatives of workers who came from their own workforces.

Not all unions followed this strategy. In particular, the newer community unions recruited at general meetings in the townships and handed out leaflets in the street inviting people to join. Anyone who signed was entered as a union member even if he or she paid no further subscriptions and did not proclaim union membership while at work. Other unions were meticulous in refusing to recruit beyond what they perceived to be their organisational capacities even if that resulted in the union having only a small membership.

Key role of shop stewards

Great emphasis is placed on company-by-company, workplace-by-workplace organisation. By 1983, four unions affiliated to FOSATU covering the metal, textile, transport and chemical industries had organised 321 factories and negotiated recognition agreements in 226 of these. FOSATU has published a 72-page booklet entitled 'The Shop Steward'. Half of it is an historical account of the British shop steward movement with upbeat accounts of the strength of shop stewards during the First World War or at Ford plants in Britain in the 1960s. The booklet goes on to say that what FOSATU unions want from employers should be:

> RECOGNISED Shop Steward Committees. Shop Stewards represent an ORGANISATION that is PERMANENT and does not depend on individuals or management.
>
> This is because they are:
> - elected by their fellow workers as representatives;
> - elected in such a way that all workers either in a section, department or shift have a representative that they can contact;
> - governed by constitutional rules that allow members to replace them if they do not perform their duties;
> - supported by the Union who can train them, give them advice and assistance and support them in dealing with grievances or negotiations;
> - linked to their fellow workers in other factories through their Union and through their federation of Unions.
>
> Shop Stewards are:
> - representatives of workers;
> - elected department by department;

● elected according to the union constitution;
● trained to perform their duties by the union;
● linked to other worker leadership through their union and their federation of unions.

(*Source:* The Shop Steward, FOSATU).

The National Union of Mineworkers, a CUSA affiliate, has produced a 130-page training manual for its shaft stewards and tells them:

> "The Shaft Steward will succeed in uniting members if he acts in a respectful way with all members and does not try to be their boss. He must remember that the members elected him to represent them because they had confidence in him. He must also remember that if he does not serve them satisfactorily they can always remove him from his position.
>
> The Shaft Steward is the leader of the workers in the work place. Members will always look to him for leadership in every situation that confronts them. The Shaft Steward must be prepared for this. He must be well-informed and be interested in all the things happening in his section or department. He must be willing to be trained by the union to increase his knowledge so that he can impart his knowledge to other workers."

Finding effective shopfloor leaders is a problem as Joe Foster, responsible during the 1970s for organising workers at the Leyland factory in Cape Town, noted: "You call for elections and no-one puts his name down, so you go and ask someone and he says no, and you try to persuade him and so on. And then when you get a new shop steward you have to train him. At the moment we have a whole lot of new shop stewards but we don't just tell them about the workers' rights and legislation. We also educate them about the capitalist system and imperialism and what we are struggling for in South Africa . . . Workers' control is a long and difficult process, you can't just walk in and have everyone participating. But that's what the struggle is all about."

In the Hendred Fruehof factory which makes lorry trailers near Johannesburg, 95 per cent of the 400 workers belong to the Metal and Allied Workers Unions, MAWU. Each department — paint-shop, tank-shop, stores etc — elects one shop steward and an alternate. There are no full-time shop stewards. The chairman of the shop stewards is John Nonjeka, a 43-year-old welder. The stewards meet every Wednesday and hold a general meeting once a fortnight to which all members may come.

Branches and locals

This relentless participatory democracy continues on up through the MAWU structure. Like most South African unions with a membership extending beyond one geographical area MAWU has branches corresponding more or less to the major regions in the country. So there are four MAWU branches for Transvaal, South and North Natal and the Eastern Cape. Branches are further sub-divided into locals, offices from which full-time organisers work. The MAWU office at Katlehong in the East Rand, to which the Hendred Fruehof factory is attached, is a shabby, brick hall behind a garage. Rows of benches provide the seating and there are two desks, one with a telephone and typewriter, the other pushed against a wall to make way for a meeting. These local offices are where shop stewards' councils meet. These *ad hoc* bodies have helped organise workers by launching recruitment drives. At the beginning of 1981, in the area around the Katlehong local, there were only two factories in which FOSATU unions were organised. By the end of 1981, shop stewards from 23 factories representing 7,000 workers were attending shop stewards' council meetings. Unions affiliated to FOSATU help each other with office facilities or, as in Port Elizabeth, have a kind of general suite of offices and meeting rooms which all FOSATU affiliates may use. The same is true of CUSA unions and the head offices of the main CUSA unions are situated in the same office building in Johannesburg.

Each factory elects one delegate and an alternate to the branch executive committee of MAWU. So with 77 factories in Transvaal, the branch executive is 150 strong. In turn, each branch elects four delegates and two alternates to provide a 24-strong National Executive Committee for the unions. Each branch holds an annual general meeting. Four thousand attended the 1983 Transvaal MAWU annual meeting which was held in a stadium.

For the National Union of Mineworkers, the organisational structure is similar, though based on shafts and mines, with each mine constituting a branch and a group of mines coming together to form regional shaft stewards' councils and regional committees. Regional loyalties are important and sometimes there can be fierce divisions between different region-based branches of the same union. In 1984, MWASA, the media workers' union, effectively split when the Western Cape branch affiliated to the United Democratic Front against the wishes of the Transvaal and Natal branches. The differences between SAAWU branches in East London and in Durban contributed to that union's grave internal problems in 1984. Distances are so great and local political, industrial relations and leadership customs and history so different that detailed national control can sometimes be difficult.

Full-time officials

At all levels in the emerging trade unions the emphasis on elected shopfloor workers forming local, branch and national committees is stressed. But very few unions have negotiated agreements for full-time shop stewards. The need exists for full-time organisers paid for by the union. In most unions the general (or national) secretary is appointed by the national executive council. Organisers are also appointed either by the national executive council or, for example, in MAWU's case, they may be appointed by the branch executive committee. The pay of organisers varies from union to union. In MAWU's case their 23 organisers earn R500 a month, about the same as a semi-skilled metalworker. In NAAWU, where the pay rates are the highest for black workers, organisers earn around R800 a month, while in the General Workers' Union which organises poorly paid dock and general workers the rate for an organiser is R400 a month. The National Union of Mineworkers' 17 full-time officials receive between R320 to R450 a month compared with the average pay of a miner of R264 a month. As in most unions the full-time organisers start as union activists, become elected office-bearers and apply to be full-time organisers. Most are young, under 40, and have been through a variety of strikes, dismissals and successful negotiation in the changing labour scene since 1973.

Titus McKenna was a shop steward in Leyland who became a full-time organiser for FOSATU in 1981. He was attached to the textile workers union in organising drives and has now been sent to help the paperworkers' union. David Sebabi was born in 1952 and was employed by Toyota as a clerical worker. He became a full-time organiser with MAWU in 1979, and was appointed general secretary in 1981. Three years later he left that post and became an organiser again. In fact, there is quite a turnover in many FOSATU unions in the post of general secretary. In part this may be self-preservation. Some emerging unions whose general secretaries have adopted high public profiles have become the object of state repression. In addition, changes in the composition of the executive committee can result in a general secretary being ousted following a shift in the balance of power. In some of the labour writings in South Africa there are warnings about entrenched union bureaucracies emerging that gradually win control of a union and then cease to be accountable to workers.

White organisers

An important difference between the FOSATU and CUSA unions is over the role of white organisers. The NUM's handbook for shaft stewards says that one of the fundamental principles of the the union is "black worker leadership". In contrast a brochure published by the National Union of Textile Workers states: "We hire organisers according to their ability and not according to their race". Some of the more dynamic black unions such as the General Workers Union and the Food and Canning Workers' Union have long had white general secretaries, David Lewis and Jan Theron respectively.

John Copelyn has been general secretary of the National Union of Textile Workers since his appointment by the executive council in 1982. While a student at university in Johannesburg he became involved in the union movement during the strike wave of 1973. He worked as a union organiser until 1976 when he was banned. He qualified as a lawyer during his three-and-a-half years of being banned and once that was lifted came straight back to work for the union. "Until 1983, I was the only white. Now we have appointed two more, an organiser and our health and safety officer", Copelyn explained. Standing beside the union president, Gain Ngqawana, a full-time shop steward at Industrex, a Belgian-owned fabric plant in Port Elizabeth, Copelyn said that he did not have that direct a rapport with the membership. "I'm stuck in head office preparing legal papers and educational material with a lot of administration and financial work for the branches. We have computerised membership and financial records for our 19,000 members at the head office in Durban", he said.

Some white general secretaries have tried to avoid having too outspoken a role in their unions. Others, like David Lewis, have written extensively about the theory and history of black trade unions. Neil Aggett's death underlined the influential role played by whites in the development of the emerging unions since 1973. The contemptuous term 'white academic' is to be found on the lips of both employers and old-style union leaders as they denounce what they see as manipulation by outsiders. It is a point raised with rather more seriousness by those who argue that workers' organisations should have workers holding all the posts, especially an important one like that of general secretary which, however one down-plays it, is a key union position. Calvin Nkbabinde, general secretary of a small blacks-only engineering union based in Johannesburg, said: "The black man is pushed according to his needs, the white sympathiser according to his ideology. The black man has been so used to deferring to the white. A white union organiser tends to be more and more relied on." In contrast, David Madutela, an executive council member of MAWU, which has three white organisers claimed: "The white intellectuals should be used. We can learn from them. But we must take that learning and put it into use ourselves. If we make mistakes so be it. In the factories shop stewards have to learn to stand on their own feet.

Workers still ask the whites to come and do the negotiating." His point was echoed by Andrew Zulu, vice-president of FOSATU, who said: "The whites are there as advisers. That's where they should stay. We have to provide the leadership. Sometimes the white intellectuals go too far in offering leadership and then there is the possibility of a clash."

Recruitment

Whites only play a limited personal role in recruitment. One of the organisers' key tasks is recruiting. Often one of the African languages is needed, especially amongst migrant workers. Volkswagen's John Gomomo, for example, can speak English, Afrikaans, Zulu, Xhosa and can understand Tswana (in passing, one might ask how many union movements in the world throw up worker leaders fluent in four languages) and it is normal for union meetings to be conducted in more than one language. The normal method of recruitment is to meet small groups of workers and persuade them to join the union and recruit their fellow workers. Sometimes the unions are awash with membership applications. More than 7,000 workers in different factories applied to join MAWU in Natal during the rolling wave of engineering factory disputes. MAWU was identified as standing out against the Industrial Council wage offer and demanding a much higher minimum wage. Once a union has recruited more than 40 per cent of the workers in a factory it can apply for recognition. Msoks Qotole, an organiser with the General Workers Union, described the problems they had at a Cape Town factory, once the union arrived with sufficient signed forms to begin negotiation over recognition. "The management interviews each worker and asks him if he is sure he knows what kind of form he has signed to join the union. The personnel officer, who also referred to the workers as "the boys" clearly didn't believe they could write. The word in Xhosa for subscription is 'Irhafu' which can also mean payment or tax. So when a worker was asked if he knew he had paid 'Irhafu' the white personnel man who speaks Xhosa says, "Ah, ha. So you pay tax. What's that got to do with the union?" The workers just replied patiently, "Yes, it's 'Irhafu' for the union."

How unions are financed

Union subscriptions also vary from union to union, and amount on average to about 0.75 per cent of the weekly wage. The National Union of Mineworkers' subscription is R1 a month, that of the Metal and Allied Workers' Union, R2 per month. In the NUM's case the money is collected by shaft stewards and after being divided between local and national use is sent on to the head office. Many of the industrial unions have negotiated check-off or stop-order systems so that the union subscription is automatically deducted from the members' wages and forwarded by the employer to the union. The money is used to pay salaries, run offices, pay benefits, publish education material and leaflets and even to help organisers with car driving lessons. The National Automobile and Allied Workers' Union arranges for each of its officials to have a car through a complicated leasing system. But MAWA's 23 organisers only have four union cars between them so valuable time is lost as one organiser chauffeurs another to a meeting.

Workers are also compensated for lost pay when they have to take working days off to attend meetings. Those attending a 2-day meeting of the Chemical Workers Industrial Union National Executive Committee held at Wilgespruit in Transvaal in February 1984 found themselves discussing issues such as who to employ as an organiser, an allegation that the vice-president was not performing his duties satisfactorily, a rise in subscription rates, co-operation with a rival union, a report from the FOSATU executive committee and reports from the general secretary and from the branches.

As always the dry recorded minutes of such meetings conceal as much as they disclose, but any trade union activist or official from Britain, the rest of Europe or North America would find plenty of common ground in the work and organisation of the South African unions. In Britain, much heat is generated over the closed shop, which British unions correctly see, in the British economic and political context, as an essential collective defence against the power of employers. In South Africa, the closed shops granted to the white dominated unions have been used to perpetuate control over black workers who were barred from forming their own unions. Management came to agreements with such unions and workers even find themselves having subscriptions deducted without their consent. So the rivalries between unions over organisation and jurisdiction rights has been marked. It is not just between white and black unions, or between TUCSA and FOSATU and CUSA unions but the rivalry extended to unions with broadly the same political outlook under black leadership. It also exists between the so-called industrial and so-called community unions, between those that have registered and those that refuse to register, between those on industrial councils and those outside the industrial council system. Bearing in mind that the vast majority of black industrial workers remain to be organised, the charges of simply recruiting members from one union into another are serious.

One European metalworkers leader with more than 40 years' experience of organising returned from a visit to South Africa in 1984 and said: "Sometimes I get the impression they are shuffling the same members around. As much time is spent complaining about each others raiding activities as getting out and organising new members." Most Western union movements have agreed procedures to prevent that kind of futile inter-union rivalry. In South Africa, the frustrations and lack of trust stemming from two decades of organisational difficulties combine with deep-rooted differences over ideology to make united organisation drives impossible. Perhaps the most important union activity is the meeting. Yet even to hold meetings presents problems. In theory, whites need permission to go into black townships. Many township union meetings are held out of doors. Yet, any gathering of more than 10 people in public should have prior permission from the authorities. Transport problems for migrant workers means it is difficult to attend meetings held any distance from their hostels.

The remarkable thing about the level of organisation and the structures that have evolved is not that here and there they have their faults, but that given the difficulties against which the emerging unions have to operate they have nonetheless developed forms that blend the requirement for leadership, and full-time organisation and yet stay close to the needs of the members and the principle of democratic control and accountability.

Communications

In a large, slightly chaotic office in a Durban suburb, Ian Bissell sat one Saturday morning trying to work out what he could spike for the next issue of *Fosatu Workers' News*. Like all trade union editors he had to juggle between the demands of industrial news, longer articles, theoretical pieces and interviews with union activists. Bissell is a young Durban journalist appointed in 1983 as full-time editor of the FOSATU newspaper. It is tabloid size, with a pacy layout and a sophisticated use of headlines and photographs. Fifty thousand copies are printed every five weeks. The five-week rhythm is to circumvent a law which requires the registration of any journal appearing 12 times or more a year. Registration means the payment of a R20,000 deposit which is forfeited if the publication is banned. The May 1984 issue had 12 pages, had articles on the metal industry national wage negotiations, May Day appeals, an appeal to workers not to vote in the elections to coloured and Indian parliaments, an account of women workers' problems, the sixth part of a history of the South African working class, reports of individual union successes in food, transport, timber, textile, tyre and sugar industries, and an extract from a story about a workers' life written by Alfred Qabula, a Dunlop worker. *Fosatu Workers News* also appears in Zulu.

CUSA publishes a smaller journal, *Izwilethu*, which is A4 size with a 20,000 print run. The Commercial, Catering and Allied Workers' Union publishes *Ccawusa News* which is a four-page tabloid while the General Workers' Union publishes, irregularly, *Phambili Basebenzi*. The Metal and Allied Workers' Union published an A4 size newsletter *Umbiko we MAWU*.

In addition to newspapers many of the emerging unions produce leaflets, brochures and longer booklets. CUSA publishes an occasional newsletter, *Know Your Rights* which deals with labour legislation. FOSATU's publications include such titles as *A Guide to Wage Bargaining, Why Your Union Needs Shop Stewards, Reform or Control: the New South African Labour Dispensation, Fighting Retrenchment, International Trade Unionism, Unemployment Insurance Fund* and *Workmen's Compensation*. Academics and writers sympathetic to the black unions have also helped produce short booklets on aspects of South Africa trade union history. These are written in clear, direct language. In Cape Town, a trade union library for workers has been opened.

The need to improve direct union communication with members and the communities in which they live is important as the media in South Africa, as elsewhere, is biased against the workers and their unions. Most South African companies employ public relations consultants, usually former journalists with good contacts in the press, to put over their case. During the Leyland strike in 1981, the company inserted large advertisements in the newspapers thanking strike-breakers for coming to work. In the strike at BMW near Pretoria in January 1984, the West German-owned company hired an helicopter to shower the township with leaflets inviting workers and their families to a video showing and free drinks, to put over the company's arguments. Against this, the unions are increasing their contacts with the press. All are becoming proficient in using press releases at a national level, though a traditional union-media distrust still exists. A major problem is that the South African television and radio networks are firmly under government control and the activities or views of the black workers are simply not heard.

Training and education

Increasing emphasis is now being placed on training and education for workers and those holding elected office. The National Union of Mineworkers has produced a 180-page training manual for its shaft stewards. The union has also appointed a full-time education officer. A 1979 FOSATU booklet, *Factory Research,* states: "Research is not something special which can only be done by intellectuals or people with degrees. Every organiser and every worker can help with research."

In 1983, FOSATU appointed a full-time education secretary, Alex Erwin, who has organised a series of labour studies courses, lasting for one or two weeks. A two-week-long education workshop was held in and around Johannesburg in July 1983. Lectures included such subjects as 'Workers and Democracy', 'Workers and the Community' and 'Women Workers'. More than 300 workers attended these courses.

Individual unions organise courses for shop stewards, local and branch officers. The subjects cover subjects from the mundane, if important, such as basic bookkeeping and office administration, to public speaking, wage bargaining, labour law and political economy. In 1983, in Natal, FOSATU and its affiliates organised 32 education courses attended by 842 workers; in Transvaal, 23 courses were attended by 1,636 participants. The Federation has begun using video cassettes to teach workers about grievance procedures. With a legal studies centre, the union has jointly produced a series of short plays which show how ill-informed shop stewards can mess up the handling of a workers' grievance and then how to do it properly.

To attend a black workers' meeting in South Africa is to hear songs and chants interspersed with the serious union business. At all important regional and national meetings, workers' choirs compete with each other in front of the crowd. Workers also stage plays about factory life. One of them staged by Dunlop workers has this line from a worker who is allowed to be an austronaut for the day: "You know, I'm sure if I came to live on the moon, Dunlop would start a factory just to torment me. And Vorster would come up just to make sure I carry a pass."

Chapter 6

Workers Health and Safety Becomes an Issue

On Monday 12 September 1983 the morning shift at the state-owned Hlobane colliery in Natal got ready to go underground. Down in the shaft, miners shuffled to their various work posts, each reluctantly adjusting to the week's work that lay ahead. Various machines used underground were switched on. One of them, a scoop that drags the coal along to dumper trucks, seemed to be short-circuiting. It was a normal enough sight and the miners had almost got used to the electric flashes from the poorly maintained equipment. What no-one knew that morning was that over the weekend a large quantity of methane gas had seeped into the area where the men were beginning the day's shift. Of all the dangers coalminers face methane is perhaps the greatest. It is odourless and colourless. An uncomplicated hydrocarbon, the simplest member of the paraffin series, methane hugs the ceiling of mine shafts. Going into a mine full of methane is like walking into a sealed room a metre deep in paraffin. When a spark or an electrical flash touches it, the effect is instant incineration. That's what happened at Hlobane when the electric sparks from the scoop ignited the methane gas. Sixty-four miners were burnt alive. Four more died after days of agony in hospital and several were seriously injured.

A build-up of methane gas is a normal, indeed predictable mining danger. It is avoided by adequate ventilation and by checks before work begins to ensure that the area is methane free. In addition, according to South African government regulations, underground machinery is meant to be flame-proof. None of these conditions were met at Hlobane. A few days before the explosion there had been major holing operations which had not been properly sealed off, which meant that the mine's ventilation system did not clear away the methane. One miner had reported the presence of methane but the mine management decided he was lying to cover up a poor production record. Only four out of the required ten flame safety lamps were in operation in the area of the blast. Of those, only one had a probe attachment necessary to test for methane on the mine ceiling. Of 29 machines in the blast area, 14 were not flame proof and could have caused the explosion.

A detailed enquiry into the Hlobane tragedy revealed other

examples of management indifference and the lack of effective
regulation, inspection and enforcement of safety procedures. But
one fact emerged above all from the events surrounding the blast:
that the miners themselves had no say in safety procedures and that
their union had no legal or contractual right to intervene on their
behalf. The responsibility for the health and safety of the worker in
South Africa rests entirely with the employer.

The way employers have discharged this responsibility can be
measured by South Africa's workplace accidents which are
amongst the highest in the world. In the 1980s, according to the
governments' Workmens' Compensation Commission, there were
an average 300,000 accidents at work each year, with 2,000 deaths
and 30,000 workers left permanently disabled. There is little safety
training and much unsafe machinery. More than 90 per cent of the
accidents in coal mines were officially blamed on 'acts of God',
whereas management and workers are blamed for fewer than 2 per
cent.

In 1983, a total of 831 miners died in accidents, three quarters of
them in gold mines, South Africa's main source of wealth. Between
1972 and 1982, 8,209 miners were killed in gold, coal and other
mines. Even these statistics were challenged as being too modest.
According to Dr Herbert Eisner, the former head of the explosives
and flame laboratory of the British Health and Safety Executive,
the methods used by the South African government in gathering
statistics on mining accidents are no longer considered reliable by
other important mining countries. The mining death rate in South
Africa was six times that of the United Kingdom, he said.

The NUM steps in

The issue of miners' safety has become a priority for the black
National Union of Mineworkers (NUM), according to its president,
Cyril Ramophosa. Several resolutions on safety were passed at the
NUM's second annual conference held in December 1983. The
union has demanded that its safety stewards be fully recognised by
the Chamber of Mines. Six months before the Hlobane disaster the
NUM had applied to join the official Mines Safety Committee, but
their application was turned down by the Government Mining
Engineer who said the union was 'unrepresentative'. The NUM has
70,000 members and many miners not yet in the union followed its
call for a 30 minutes stoppage in protest at the Hlobane tragedy.
The NUM is now insisting on being legally represented at all
enquiries into mining disasters. It also won an important legal case
when the Industrial Court backed 17 NUM members who refused to
work in an area they thought unsafe in a West Driefontein mine.

Management of Gold Fields, the company which owns the mine, fired the workers but the court ordered that they be reinstated. After the case the NUM said it would advise its members that they had the right to refuse to go into areas they thought unsafe and the union called on mine owners to conclude safety agreements with it in order to avoid court actions. The NUM has also flown in safety experts from other countries to advise in improvements in mine safety procedures.

Accidents are not the only hazard workers have to face. Cancer- or disease-inducing substances and chemicals are in common use in many production processes. Workers are also exposed to dangers such as high noise levels, fumes, dust, mineral fibres, solvents, sprays, paints and other toxins. The West German government, for example, recognises 280 high risk substances workers should avoid exposure to: in the United States the figure is also 280. Even Czechoslovakia lists 70. The latest number of high risk substances recognised by South Africa is just 49.

Shift work, unless properly controlled by a union-management agreement, can also harm a worker's overall health. A survey of cleaners working at night in Johannesburg offices showed that 64 per cent had only two to four hours sleep a day. This was caused partly by the nature of the shift work, partly by the vibration of the cleaning machines, which meant they found if difficult to sleep easily when at home. Four out of five women complained of sore eyes and headaches and nearly half were diagnosed as suffering from high blood pressure. None of the workers was in a union.

50,000 workers at risk from asbestos

Barry Castleman is one of the United States' best known experts on workplace health and safety. He has advised the US Congress, the International Labour Organisation and numerous North American unions on the issue. Castleman toured South African factories and mines in 1983 to look into safety conditions. He described the experience as "like going back in a time machine". He saw welders using blow torches without face shields, miners pouring molten gold without safety glasses and workers in dangerously high noise areas without ear protection. Castleman was especially scathing about the protection given the workers handling asbestos. Ten thousand workers are employed in South African asbestos mines and a further 40,000 workers handle asbestos directly as part of their daily job.

Everite is South Africa's largest manufacturer of fibre-cement and other products containing a mixture of blue and white asbestos fibre and cement. The company is a subsidiary of the Swiss Eternit group. In South Africa, Everite employs 24,200 workers in four plants. Only in the last few years has the company started to organise health checks for its employees. In 1983, as a result of these and subsequent union pressure, 23 workers at one of Everite's plants in Cape Town were retired early on full pay after it was diagnosed that they suffered from asbestosis, a serious — often fatal — lung disease caused by exposure to asbestos.

At the time of the men's retirement, the workers' union, the General Workers' Union, was still in the middle of trying to get the company to agree to a recognition agreement. GWU general secretary, David Lewis, had asked the company at least to co-operate with the union over health matters but Everite had refused to agree to this. The union had plenty of points to raise. The 23 men had not been moved to lower exposure areas after being certified as having asbestosis. An inspection of the plant showed that workers handling raw asbestos mixed with water and cement were doing so without masks. Workers were to be seen cutting asbestos sheets without masks.

Dr Jonathan Myers, of the University of Cape Town's industrial health research unit, has taken a particular interest in the dangers of asbestos and in the Everite case. Everite claims that over 37 years only 71 workers out of 24,200 have been diagnosed as having asbestosis, an average of 0.29 per cent. Of those only 15 have died from asbestos-related diseases. Dr Myers finds it difficult to accept these figures: "According to international studies of workers in asbestos product plants in other parts of the world, there is nowhere where the fatalities are so low." These studies, carried out according to International Labour Organisation specifications, show the lowest rate of asbestosis to be 8.5 per cent at a fibre cement factory in Barcelona, where workers were exposed to the fibres for an average of seven years.

Dr Myers was also concerned about the level of asbestos fibres Everite permitted to be in the air. Tiny asbestos fibres, difficult to see under the microscope, are believed to cause lung cancer and mesothelioma, a rare and extremely unpleasant cancer of the lining of the lung. Sweden and Norway have completely banned the production or handling of asbestos because of its known dangers. In Britain, the maximum legal level is 0.2 fibres per ml of air, though many unions and health experts believe that any exposure to any level of asbestos fibres is dangerous. Everite's management said their workers were exposed to 1 fibre per ml of air — five times the British level.

One of the men obliged to take early retirement is Christian Mattee who had worked at the factory for 30 years. For eight years he loaded raw asbestos dust from a train. Then he became a tractor driver which also involved loading asbestos. "In 1977, they told me I had something in my lungs. I carried on working as a tractor driver until November 1983, when I was transferred."

The workers' fears about the daily danger they face has undoubtedly helped the union's organisation drive. Like unions facing the asbestos problem in other countries GWU's Lewis has had to adopt a twin-track policy of calling for research on substitute products which would eliminate the need for asbestos while also pressing the company for "short-term solutions: constant monitoring and very early identification of the disease, protective clothing and a monitoring of the production".

Campaigning against 'Brown Lung'

Another union that has taken up the question of workers' health with great effect is the National Union of Textile Workers (NUTW). In 1981, the union began testing textile workers for 'brown lung' disease (known medically as *byssinosis*). This is a well-known disease caused by cotton dust. It first came to prominence as a major industrial disease in the United States in the 1970s after union campaigns secured compensation for several hundred workers affected by 'brown lung'.

In South Africa, the NUTW had tested thousands of workers and produced pamphlets, leaflets and posters alerting their members to the dangers of cotton dust exposure. In 1983, one union member, John Hlela became the first black worker to be awarded a lump sum and a pension of R109 after the Bureau of Occupational Diseases had accepted that his disability was caused by cotton dust induced 'brown lung'. In 1984, three more workers won payments and were awarded pensions.

The fight to secure financial compensation for workers whose future lives are probably shortened, certainly blighted, by having contracted industrial diseases is more than retrospective action on the part of the union. The examples serve to encourage other workers to be alert to the dangers and to insist they are taken up with management. In 1983 the NUTW appointed a full-time health and safety officer, a physician, Dr Neil White, and has started to keep medical records of their members. NUTW general secretary, John Copelyn, said it was important "to build up medical records of our members even if they have clear lungs when first tested, so that if five years later the worker finds he has lung disease, the union will have proof that it was caused by the factory."

The question of dust levels, he said, had always been considered the "unchallenged prerogative of management" but now plant union committees were taking up this issue. They had also demanded extra hazard payments for having to work in dusty areas and insisted the workers should be transferred to dust-free working environments if they felt unwell.

The Food and Canning Workers Union (FCWU) has also taken up the question of its members health. In 1982, workers at a fruit drying factory in Montagu, near Cape Town were worried about one of the chemicals used. This was sodium metabisulphate which is mixed with the fresh fruit and helps to preserve its colour during the drying process. However as the fruit goes through a quick drying tunnel the chemical dissolves giving off sulphur dioxide gas which can cause a variety of physical, mainly respiratory complaints as well as nausea and dizziness. The union carried out tests on its members which showed a high level of problems connected with working near the drying tunnels giving off these fumes. In 1983, the FCWU approached the management simply, at that stage, to discuss the problem. The management response was to announce that it was going to scale down the operation and that henceforth fruit would be dried in the traditional way, that is outside in the sun. But this meant that the factory's designation was changed to that of a farm. Workers were laid off and although the union's health and safety worries were obliquely met, the need for strong union organisation in the first place was underlined.

Anger over company medical schemes

In the propaganda they offer to the outside world many South African companies boast about health schemes they have set up and also claim to provide free or cheap medical services for their workers. One such is the De Beers diamond company in Kimberley. It says that the company doctor provides free medical advice; there is a hospital paid for by De Beers and a cheap medical scheme to which workers can belong to provide a wide range of medical services for themselves and their families.

Shop stewards belonging to the mining union organising at De Beers tell a very different story. They say that a black worker who felt unwell first had to get permission from the foreman, who made a prior examination before he was allowed to go to the company hospital. Then he sees a nursing sister who decides whether he can see the doctor. Even if admitted into the hospital there is pressure to report back for work. The company doctor, who was also a director of De Beers, urged workers to join the company medical scheme which cost R30 per month. He refused to refer workers to their own, black doctors. An attempt by four black doctors to set up in practice was thwarted by the town council (over which De Beers has immense influence as Kimberley for the last century has, more or less, been a company town) which refused the black doctors permission to open surgeries in the town centre. One union activist described how several years ago he called up the De Beers company doctor because his baby son was sick. He made the call at 7.30am after the baby had been up all night. The doctor eventually arrived at 9.30 in the evening. He gave a prescription but the dispensary was shut until the following morning. During the night the little boy died. Other workers complain that they could not afford the R30 a month to join the company medical scheme. Of all the issues discussed at a general union meeting of De Beers' shop stewards in March 1984 the problems of medical treatment, and of workers not being made to work when they felt unwell, took up most of time. The stewards were angry in their condemnation of the company.

New safety legislation under fire

All the independent unions are united in their criticism of the 1983 Machinery and Occupational Safety Act. At first sight it looks progressive. But as with other recent South African workplace legislation it flatters to deceive. Employers are obliged to set up Health and Safety Committees in their factories and appoint Safety Representatives. But the decision on who should be a Safety Representative is entirely for management and the committees are under management control. The new Act lays down that the employer will appoint worker representatives to the health and safety committee and will draw up its agenda and chair its meetings. Managements are encouraged by the government to appoint supervisory personnel as Safety Representatives, and they will have no special training, no right to information and no powers to enforce decisions made by the Health and Safety Committees. The new law does not list hazardous materials to which workers should not be exposed. Factory inspectors have to make several inspection visits before they can take action, thus leaving employers plenty of time to cover their tracks. Unlike the norm in most Western countries, which makes the employer liable to prosecution for failing to enforce safety precautions, there is even a provision in the Act permitting employers to dismiss workers who do not wear protective clothing.

In response to the new Act, unions in FOSATU said they would nominate their own shop stewards to sit on Health and Safety Councils and strongly oppose employers who try to nominate their own Safety Representatives. As the 1983 FOSATU annual report noted: "the experience was that bargaining over health and safety was very difficult in an environment that still required a struggle for basic recognition rights.'' However FOSATU and other independent unions have successfully begun to give health and safety in the workplace a much higher profile. Doctors and research institutes are now paying more attention to workers' health problems and unions from Europe and North America have been sending industrial health and safety officials to help South African unions with training courses and expert advice.

But it is workers themselves who will be the force to secure safer workplace environments. One of the pamphlets put out in South Africa as part of the 'brown lung' campaign sums it up thus:

"Most workers see illness as a personal problem. They see illness as something that can be cured by a doctor. And, if they are badly affected they think they can get compensation. But this is not the solution. Doctors cannot cure or prevent this illness. Compensation does not make factories safer. It is only through organisation that workers can learn about this illness and begin the struggle to make the factories safer and prevent this illness. Prevention is better than cure.''

Chapter 7

Women Workers Assert Their Rights

The problems facing black women workers in South Africa, like those faced by their counterparts in Europe, America and Asia, go beyond the workplace difficulties arising from the struggle between labour and capital, go beyond even the nature of racial repression inherent in South Africa and touch upon the life that women have to live subordinate to men, within the family and society itself. As Gloria Barry, a General Motors worker in Port Elizabeth for 10 years before she began work full-time for the union, said: ''I believe that very few males ever accepted that women are in equal partnership with them as the creator of man and, as such, of labour power that ensures that the planet Earth continues to develop in the hands of the male species.''

The widespread practice of 'lobola', a payment made by a would-be husband to the family of the woman he wishes to marry, confers an almost chattel status on the wife. Unions holding meetings for women workers have had to write to husbands, asking politely for permission for the wife to attend the meeting and assuring the husband that his wife would be participating in serious union business.

In Soweto, six out of 10 children do not have married parents and the single working mother is a common phenomenon. In Soweto, there are 90,000 pre-school children, but only one centre for those under the age of two. For most working women, there is an exhausting routine — 'the dual shift' — of housework, cooking, childcare and sexual provision to be added to a day's work. Yet, at the same time the changing nature of women's participation in manufacturing and service industries and their increasing activity in the trade union movement mean that women are challenging the daily oppression they have to live with.

More women enter workforce
The shift from agricultural labour and domestic service into waged employment has been quite marked, though it needs to be set in context — according to the 1980 census nearly four out of five African women were said to be 'not economically active', and 57 per cent live in the bantustans where waged employment is rare for

both women and men. Nonetheless, that leaves 1.7 million African women workers. In 1946 African women constituted only 1.8 per cent of all production workers in South Africa; by 1982 12.8 per cent of African women were employed in production work. They work mainly in semi-skilled or unskilled jobs and are a concentration in the textile and food industries. In 1981, women constituted 46.8 per cent of workers in the textile industry, and of those 64.9 per cent were African women.

**Percentage increase of women in the black work-force by sector,
1973-1981**

Sector/Industry	Percentage increase
Shoe	23.9
Commerce	15.2
Electrical machinery	15.0
Textile	12.1
Clothing	7.2
Non-metal mineral	3.6
Food	3.5
Furniture	2.9
Chemical	2.0
Wood	2.9

(*Source:* National Manpower Surveys)

Female wages are low. Although the government has repealed legislation permitting wage discrimination, employers still pay women less than men. In the Transvaal clothing industry in 1982, a female sewing machinist earned 50 per cent less (R33) than a male sewing machinist (R49.50).

There has been a steady shift of women into wage labour in the service sector. In 1946, 93.1 per cent of all women service workers were domestic servants. By 1980, only one third of African women in paid employment were in service work. In a sense, the externally employed service work does not differ that much from domestic service — it still consists of cleaning, laundry, cooking and waitress work. But this expanding sector (from 62,468 in 1973 to 112,024 in 1981) has helped increase the possibility of union organisation and the raising of women workers' consciousness through their own agitation and industrial activity.

Fighting for maternity rights

That such union organisation is badly needed can be seen by looking at how South African capital and the state respond to what to them is perhaps the most important function of women relative to the labour force — that of reproducing it. "If you get pregnant, that's it, they fire you." That's how a Transvaal woman shop steward summed up one of the main problems facing women workers. In a chemical firm, women workers had to sign a document stating: "I, the undersigned, hereby declare that I am not pregnant. I furthermore agree that should I fall pregnant in the next 12 months, my services should be terminated immediately." All forms of contraception are used, including the controversial Depo Provera drug, which is injected in employer-run clinics. Back street abortions are frequent. An industrial relations officer at Kellogs said: "In a place where I worked before, a woman who was pregnant wrapped her stomach tightly so that no-one would know she was pregant because she was afraid of losing her job. This made her abort." Another women said she wore outsize dustcoats at work in order to disguise her pregnancy.

During pregnancy, retail workers reported that they were moved away from shop counters, as management did not want them to have contact with the public. A Commercial, Catering and Allied Workers' Union organiser said that a pregnant shop assistant may be moved into warehouse work which is often arduous and involves carrying crates or climbing ladders, precisely the kind of activity a pregnant woman should avoid.

Even in those companies which permit their women employees leave to have babies, the financial pressure to return to work is strong. For even if a woman worker has paid for three years into the state Unemployment Insurance Fund she can claim only about one-third of her wages for 18 weeks before and eight weeks after confinement.

South African labour law provides little protection for women. Indeed, the 1983 Basic Condition of Employment Act actually removed certain protections that women had in respect of overtime and nightwork. By contrast, the law obliges companies to give white male workers generous time off for military training and their jobs and fringe benefits are protected during such absences.

The conflict between the needs of capital and the requirements of the apartheid state emerged in the recommendations of the Wiehahn Commission. Under advanced capitalist organisation female labour is needed to fill unskilled and low-pay jobs, and women are increasingly incorporated into the labour market. Under pressure from women organised in unions, but also in response to the need to protect and keep women workers (relatively) quiescent in terms of their family and reproductive roles, most states have passed legislation aimed at protecting women's maternity rights and preventing unfair discrimination in employment or workplace practices.

Wiehahn, in trying to develop Western norms of labour legislation, was obliged to include certain recommendations in favour of women. These included equal unemployment benefits for women, a prohibition on being dismissed because of pregnancy, pre-confinement leave to be raised to six weeks, pregnancy leave earnings to go up to 60 per cent, light duties for pregnant women to be legally obligatory. The government rejected all these recommendations. To wait then for the state to grant improvements in the conditions women face at work was pointless. Instead, women workers began organising, demanding and successfully negotiating maternity and other relevant agreements, combating sexual harassment and forcing their male colleagues to discuss, albeit hesitantly, problems of sexism and patriarchy which are intertwined with apartheid and the employers' dominant position in South Africa.

Women union activists

Lydia 'Mama' Kompe is the Transvaal organiser of the Transport and General Workers' Union. She joined the Metal and Allied Workers' Union in 1974 when she worked for Heinemann Electric. "There were 606 workers in Heinemann, mostly women. In three months we managed to organise almost the entire plant. I was elected a shop steward", she said. But although the majority of the workers were women, it was men who played a commanding role in the union organisation. "At Heinemann we had six women shop stewards out of 12. This was because we were insisting and our organiser, Khubeka, was encouraging us. But our chairman was a man. During meetings we tried to fight the undermining of women's suggestions. They thought we were not saying strategic things. But we managed to fight that. If a woman stands up and puts a motion or a suggestion, it should be taken into consideration. We succeeded in Heinemann because women outnumbered men. We weren't scared even when the police were trying to thrash us and scare us with dogs. I think that was when women realised that women can be determined", said 'Mama' Kompe.

Several women have been chosen as general secretaries. Tembi Nabe was elected by the executive council of MAWU to the post in May, 1984. June-Rose Nala was also general secretary of MAWU before going to Ruskin College, Oxford on a trade union scholarship.

Other women who have held a general secretary position recently are Refilo Nzuta of the Paper, Wood and Allied Workers Union;

Maggie Magubane of the Sweet, Food and Allied Workers' Union and Emma Mashinini, who was detained for five months while general secretary of the Commercial, Catering and Allied Workers' Union. Others are full-time organisers like Aninka Claassens of the Paper, Wood and Allied Workers' Union and Rita Ndzanga, organising secretary in the General and Allied Workers' Union. In classical trade union nomenclature, the term *general secretary* has an authoritative ring and often describes the union's chief officer who occupies the post after a fiercely contested election or long service as an official. In the emerging unions, with their strong emphasis on almost day-to-day control by an executive committee elected from rank and file workers, the role of the general secretary is far less authoritative and, in FOSATU unions, for example, there has been a fair turnover of general secretaries. As 'Mama' Kompe noted, the crucial power-broking leadership positions are still dominated by men: "No union has yet elected a branch chairlady. Offhand, I don't know even of a chairlady of a shop stewards committee. Perhaps a female treasurer, since people think a woman is more responsible and will be more careful with money. Even the women feel it's important to elect men. I don't know why. Even in textiles, where there's mostly women, I've never heard of a chairlady of the branch or a president."

At a conference organised by FOSATU to discuss problems arising from organising women workers, the question of the extra burden of housework and child-rearing was raised by several women shop stewards. MAWU general secretary Tambi Nebe described the unequal division of labour in the home thus:

"Both man and wife have to get up in the morning to work. But the woman has to get up first; make tea for her husband, prepare water to wash, make the bed while the man is washing; wash the baby and take it to the nurse lady who looks after it. Then she comes home and prepares herself to go to work.

"But remember the woman works as a domestic, harassed by the madam the rest of the day. Or she works in a factory. Long hours. Hard work. She finishes work at 5.30pm and then she has to travel from work to home. The earliest she can get home is 7.30pm.

"The husband also finishes work at about 5.30pm. When he gets home he doesn't make fire to make the house warm; he will just put on the heater and sit next to it, and read the paper, watch TV, or play horses. He doesn't fetch the baby. He doesn't look after it. You know, he makes it a point that every time when he comes back from work, there's this 'little darling' next to him, which is a bottle of whisky or brandy!

"On the way home from work the woman will fetch the child.

When she gets home she makes the fire, starts preparing the evening meal, then washes the child, and feeds it, and then prepares the bed for the husband. The woman must do everything — see to it that tomorrow morning she doesn't have too much work to do because she must carry the baby and prepare everything. Most women do their ironing during the night.

"And when it comes to bed time, the husband becomes impatient if the woman does not come to bed when he calls her. When she does go to bed — there starts the overtime. But if she is tired and refuses him, that is the beginning of another problem. He becomes a cheeky somebody; he will go out. And sometimes because of this 'darling' which was on the table, it gives him powers and makes him think of battering you. Or he will go out and find another woman. And that is where divorce begins."

Sexual harassment

Sexual harassment, by both white and black men in positions of workplace authority over women, is an issue that South African unions are being forced to take up by their female members. Cleaners working during the night at Anglo American offices in Johannesburg have complained about sexual abuse, especially from 'idunas', their black supervisors. A woman organiser recruiting workers in a food factory reported that a worker complained that she had not been given a wage increase by a white supervisor because she had refused to 'love' him.

At Dunlop, members of the Chemical Workers Industrial Union fought back against such sexual harassment. In a leaflet, Dunlop shop stewards explained what they did. "At Dunlop, we realised that the training officer sold jobs for sex. We planned to catch him in action with workers who could be around the offices and watch him. He employed one lady on a Friday, and by Tuesday the following week at about 1 o'clock he called the lady to his office. One of our union members rushed to the door a few minutes later to test if the door was locked or not and found it locked. He phoned another member, who phoned one of the managers. The training officer was caught 'taking his payment' and fired on the spot. The woman did not get fired."

The shop stewards concluded by noting that handling the case this way "was far better than allowing workers to assault him as they wished. We just refused, and promised them we would solve the problem. And now they are all happy." At the Unilever factory there was an even stronger reaction in April 1984 when more than 1,000 workers, members of the Food Beverage Workers Union, went on strike in protest against a white manager who was found having sex with a black female employee.

Maternity agreements

Unions have also been successful in securing some enhanced protection for women in the form of maternity agreements negotiated with employers. The Commercial, Catering and Allied Workers Union has a large female membership. The union has stipulated that maternity agreements must be signed at the same time as recognition agreements. In an agreement with one of South Africa's biggest retailing chains, OK Bazaars, CCAWUSA won the right for pregnant women to have 12 months off, without pay, before and after birth. In contrast, the Sweet Food and Allied Workers' Union has negotiated an agreement with Kellogs which provides for three months' pay while women are absent on pregnancy leave but does not guarantee them their jobs back. In May 1984, the National Automobile and Allied Workers Union secured the first ever maternity agreement in the motor industry when it negotiated 12 weeks' maternity leave at the Pretoria-based Sigma automobile manufacturer. FOSATU unions in Transvaal have formed a maternity rights group to keep the issue alive as an important trade union demand.

The struggle to secure fair play for women in the workplace can sometimes backfire. At the SA Fabrics textile factory in Durban, members of the National Union of Textile Workers, in addition to a demand for a 15 per cent wage increase, put forward a claim that the gap between male and female wages should be closed. They backed their claim with a three-day strike in February 1981. The company chose to go to arbitration, but the judge awarded a 12½ per cent increase and ordered the company to close the male-female wage gap. But the company started to lay off workers and ensured that women were the first to go. By 1983, only two women workers were left.

The organisation of women workers in South Africa is likely to face fresh problems with the arrival of new technology which may offer cost advantages to employers, especially in the textile industry, even despite the low wages paid.

As with their sisters in trade unions in countries whose labour movements pride themselves on their democratic liberties, maturity and sophistication, the women workers of South Africa are finding that in raising their natural and very necessary demands they are opening up a hitherto sealed box of prejudices that concern far more than plain economic relationships. But an essential element in the richness of the contemporary trade union scene in South Africa is precisely that women, as workers, are seeking to establish their own rights, needs, and priorities independently of, though not necessarily wholly separately from, men. 'Mama' Kompe puts it eloquently: "Why can't we be equal? What do men see us as lacking? If they could tell us what we are lacking to achieve the same rights in the union or the family, then I'd understand. But they don't give us proper reasons. Just that a woman is a woman. We pay subs equally, we work the same shifts, we work the same jobs, we participate in the same way in the unions. So I don't see why we can't have an equal say and equal rights!

"I think it's time for women to come together and see this as a major problem for us. It's a problem that will go ahead from one generation to another if we don't actually work on it. I would not like my child to grow the same as I was, as I am now. I would like my grandchildren to actually feel free, in organisations, at home, everywhere. They should have the same say, the same rights.''

Chapter 8

Industries and Unions

Automobile

Ford opened South African's first automobile factory in Port Elizabeth in 1924. Two years later, General Motors followed suit. Now the automobile and motor components industry is one of South Africa's largest, employing in 1981, 115,800 workers, of whom 71 per cent were black. The key union is the National Automobile and Allied Workers Union which organises 40 per cent of the industry's black workforce. The union was launched in the Port Elizabeth and Uitenhage area where Ford, General Motors and Volkswagen have plants. Through mergers with other unions and the opening up of branch offices in Durban (Toyota) and Transvaal (BMW, Alfa-Romeo) it has now consolidated its position throughout South Africa. NAAWU has 19,000 members.

One factor that has helped NAAWU is that the managements of most of the companies they deal with have to report to a headquarters located overseas. So NAAWU has carefully developed its relationships with the unions organising autoworkers in West Europe and North America. As long ago as 1973, NAAWU general secretary, Fred Sauls, was visiting Detroit as the guest of the United Autoworkers of America and telling the managements of Ford and General Motors that his union existed and they should tell their South African subsidiaries to negotiate with him.

The shop stewards at Volkswagen have also established a telex link with local unionists at the Volkswagen factory in Wolfsburg who are members of the 2.5 million-strong West German metalworkers' union, IG Metall. But important as these international contacts have been, the union has found itself often involved in major strikes in order to achieve its aims. In 1980, there was a prolonged stoppage involving VW workers and in 1982, 10,000 Port Elizabeth autoworkers went on strike. There were also strikes at the Leyland factory in Cape Town in 1981, during which the intervention by the British Transport and General Workers Union and the Amalgamated Union of Engineering Workers helped NAAWU's battle for recognition and better pay. The advances made by the union are illustrated by the history of organising the Leyland factory in Elandsfontein in Transvaal. This factory was originally organised by the Metal and Allied Workers Union in 1976, but the weakness of the union in those days meant that the management could brush it aside and instead come to an agreement with a TUCSA union to recruit members. After the Cape Town Leyland strike in 1981, the Transvaal workers got in touch with NAAWU and the union, in agreement with MAWU, began recruiting. Police broke up recruiting meetings and arrested a NAAWU organiser, but within a few months more than 50 per cent of the workers had joined the union and Leyland had agreed to deduct union subscriptions and hold talks for a recognition agreement.

But NAAWU is not the only union in the industry. The United African Motor and Allied Workers Union, a CUSA affiliate, won an important legal victory in 1983, when it made Nissan reinstate 102 workers the company had made redundant. Nissan also agreed to pay the workers for the earnings they had lost while retrenched. Another union organising black autoworkers is the Motor Assembly Components Workers Union based in Port Elizabeth. It has about 700 members in a Ford Cortina plant. Its former president, Thozamile Botha, was fired by the company after his involvement in a community protest boycott in Port Elizabeth. He later went into exile, but the tensions between MACWUSA and NAAWU, arising from that incident, based as they were on the conflicting priorities to be given by unions to industrial as opposed to the community struggle, have continued to this day. During the NAAWU members' strike at Ford in 1982, the Cortina plant kept working, leading to accusations of strike-breaking. There have been tentative contacts between NAAWU, the United African Motor and Allied Workers Union and a TUCSA union, the Motor Industry Combined Workers Union*, which organises mainly coloured workers, about the possibility of forming a united autoworkers' union, but no concrete proposals have emerged.

NAAWU is steadily increasing its organisation in the motor components industry. In September 1983, it pulled off the first ever strike in South Africa in which workers employed by the same company but in widely differing locations — Pretoria, Port Elizabeth and Cape Town — went on strike at the same time over the same demands. One thousand workers employed by Autoplastics went on strike simultaneously and won a wage increase.

Building and Construction

The main union for construction workers is CUSA's, Building, Construction and Allied Workers Union (BCAWU) which has

*The Motor Industry Combined Workers Union left TUCSA in July, 1984.

12,000 members. Founded in 1977, it has five regional organisers as well as a national organiser, Aaron Nthinya. In addition to the building and civil engineering industries, BCAWU, is seeking to organise in the cement, clay and ceramics factories. It has secured recognition agreements with firms such as Armitage Shanks and Johnson Tiles. Organising building workers is always extremely difficult because of the casual nature of the work, the remoteness and constantly changing location of work-sites and the willingness of employers to victimise any worker who tries to organise a union.

The union has moved slowly, consolidating its membership wherever its recruiting campaigns are successful. There have been bitter struggles at Olifantsfontein, near Pretoria. Attempts to organise in an important cermaics plant, Cullinan Industrial Porcelain, were resisted by the management. The plant was shut down for three weeks by a strike in October 1983 and when it reopened the workers were selectively rehired, with the leaders of the strike being left unemployed. Marches and demonstrations were met by police action. The workers' hotel was raided and 100 were arrested on pass offences. Other BCAWU-organised factories in the area protested to the Cullinan management and as the *Rand Daily Mail* commented at the time: "The incidents show a cohesive BCAWU presence in the area." The union was back in action early in 1984 in the same area, when a brickworks fired 16 shop stewards. This time BCAWU threatened court action on an unfair labour practices charge to get the unionists re-hired.

Other unions are also trying to organise building and construction workers, including SAAWU, the Black Allied Mining and Construction Workers Union which is linked to the black consciousness movement and, in the Western Cape, the General Workers Union. An important future area of organisation will be the civil engineering workforce where less than 1 per cent of the black workforce is unionised.

Chemical

South Africa's chemical industry dates back to the last century when the British firm ICI set up its subsidiary — African Explosives and Chemical Industries (AECI), and opened the first explosives factories to cater for the mining industry. Today, the AECI explosives plant is the world's largest. 103,000 people are employed in the chemical industry, two-thirds black, one-third white.

The most aggressive of the black unions organising in this industry is the Chemical Workers Industrial Union (CWIU) a FOSATU affiliate. Its merger with the Glass and Allied Worker

Union has given it an important foothold in the glass industry. The CUSA affiliated South African Chemical Workers Union has also been active but it would appear to have lost ground to the CWIU.

The CWIU has been particularly militant in defence of its shop stewards. When Morgan Mathebula, chairman of the shop stewards at the Cheeseborough Ponds factory, proposed a work stoppage in 1983 to commemorate the anniversary of the 1976 Soweto uprising, he was dismissed by management. Workers immediately stopped work in protest and, following further intervention by the CWIU, Mathebula was reinstated. Another attempt at a fertiliser factory in Richards Bay to dismiss two senior shop stewards was foiled by the union. In this case the management tried to manipulate disciplinary procedures to sack the two stewards but the workers made clear their willingness to strike in order to defend the two men and, in the end, they were reinstated.

The CWIU has also forced companies to open their books so that union auditors could check the financial health of a company. This happened at the G&W Industrial Minerals factory in Wadeville when 250 workers staged a two-day strike in April 1983. When the company claimed they could not afford a wage increase the workers refused to return to work until the management agreed to let union auditors inspect their books. This inspection showed that G&W had large financial reserves. The workers organised an overtime ban and this produced a substantial wage increase, with the promise of fresh wage negotiations six months later. Overtime bans and a boycott of company-run canteens were a tactic used by CWIU members in two Duropenta factories, one in Natal and one in Transvaal. Although the company had conceded a recognition agreement which gave the union plant level bargaining rights, there was pressure from the employers federation not to give wages rises above the Industrial Council minimum. The overtime ban and boycott were launched by the union to try and secure a plant level wage increase.

Overtime also became an issue at the Shatterprufe Safety Glass factory in Pretoria. There production schedules were so badly organised that one department was working short-time while others were being ordered to work extra hours. There was a factory-wide stoppage, lasting six hours, until talks between the union and management resulted in an evening out of production targets. In another Shatterprufe factory, in Port Elizabeth, workers left the TUCSA Glass Workers Union and won recognition for the CWIU with the recognition of shop stewards and the implementation of stop orders. After the signing of the recognition agreement 100 workers joined the union. According to shop steward Eddie Scholtz the arrival of the CWIU changed the atmosphere in the factory.

"Workers for the first time now have a say in their own working conditions", he said. "One of the union's first tasks would be to introduce a pension scheme", he added.

As noted elsewhere, a key area of organisation for the emerging unions are the state-owned companies. An important breakthrough has been made at SASOL, the government oil corporation which has the task of trying to reduce South Africa's dependence on imported oil by developing a way of extracting oil products from coal. In February 1984, the CWIU said it had recruited 4,000 workers at the SASOL plants in Secunda. Management had agreed to grant a stop order and discussions were continuing over a recognition agreement. If the union is successful at SASOL it will be an important breach in the general policy by 'parastatals' against the black unions. In a minor but significant victory, the CWIU managed to win the reinstatement of 36 workers dismissed by SASOL in October 1983 after they had stopped work in protest against the dismissal of a colleague. Instead of talking with the workers, the management sent in armed security police who escorted them back to their hostels. From there they were taken to different railway stations and given a one-way ticket back to their bantustans. Nearly all SASOL's African employees are migrant workers.

The CWIU took up the case and took legal action against the company. The union stated: "Workers were being treated like criminals when they were only trying to resolve a legitimate industrial grievance." The workers meanwhile had been scattered to different areas and the union had to track them down in East London, Transkei, Pongola and other places to get them to make statements. So thorough were the CWIU's preparations that in the end SASOL preferred to avoid a court case and agreed to reinstate 36 workers.

The CWIU has also won recognition agreements from the African Explosives and Chemical Industries at one of its vinyl factories at Pinetown, near Durban. Workers staged a 24-hour stoppage in protest at a low wage offer in February 1984.

Although the emerging trade union movement is dominated by affiliates of the major federations, FOSATU and CUSA, as well as the big unaffiliated and community unions, there is also a degree of spontaneous union organisation as workers hear about unions and decide to form one themselves in their factory. Hence the Black Health and Allied Workers Union (BHAWUSA) which organised the Johannesburg plant of a pharmaceutical company. BHAWUSA has no full-time office bearers and is not affiliated to any federation. Nevertheless it has extended its operation to laboratories served by the pharmaceutical plant and in March 1984

signed the first ever trade union recognition agreement with a
Johannesburg pathologists' laboratory. Again, this came after
seven months' negotiation and the threat of industrial action.

Docks

The Cape Town-based General Workers Union (GWU) has been
the main union organising dockworkers. Starting with Cape Town
stevedores, the union has gradually extended its jurisdiction up the
coast and now covers South Africa's four main ports — Cape
Town, Port Elizabeth, East London and Durban. The GWU has
won recognition agreements from the two main stevedoring
companies, South Stevedores Services and Grindrod Cotts
Stevedoring and for the stevedores — the men who load and unload
the ships — labour relations are reasonably harmonious.

The dominant force as a dockworkers' employer, however, is the
state-owned South African Transport Services (SATS) which is
violently anti-union. SATS is South African's largest employer,
with 150,000 African workers on its payroll. It has relationships
with all-white unions and other docile workers' bodies and SATS
has resisted strong efforts by the independent unions to organise
and represent workers. In the early 1980s, the General Workers
Union steadily recruited members amongst SATS employees —
mainly railway dockers who handled goods on and off trains and
lorries — in Port Elizabeth and East London. By the middle of
1982 the union had 850 members in Port Elizabeth and 350 in East
London.

Despite repeated requests, the company refused all requests for a
meeting and did not even acknowledge the signed up lists of
membership the GWU provided. Instead their reaction was one of
harassment and intimidation. SATS dismissed Jeremiah Tolwana
with 24 hours' notice saying that he was only a casual worker. In
fact, he had worked for SATS for 13 years. Tolwana was chairman
of the union committee in Port Elizabeth. Railway police detained
and interrogated other union activists, two union organisers were
arrested, workers' homes were raided and searched.

Public concern about the volatile state of labour relations in the
Port Elizabeth docks was expressed by local industrialists,
including Ford's labour relations director. Attempts by the
government Manpower Department and the International
Transport Workers Federation to intervene were brushed aside by
SATS. Finally, the Port Elizabeth workers staged a go-slow after
continuing refusal of SATS management to meet them. After first
dismissing the action as having no impact, SATS suddenly changed
its attitude and decided, early in September 1982, to break the

GWU's organisation of SATS employees. Four hundred workers were surrounded in their hostels and ordered to return to their bantustans. Attempts to organise sympathy strikes petered out as SATS refused to listen to pleas from anyone to reinstate the workers.

Having crushed, at least for the time being, efforts to organise SATS dockers, the company and the government moved to consolidate the exclusion of the GWU by passing a law in 1983 which permitted only staff associations approved by the Minister of Transport Affairs and registered as trade unions to participate in SATS conciliation machinery. SATS has set up a management-controlled Black Staff Association which is the only workers' channel for African employees. The white unions went along with this arrangement. A 1984 ILO report said this amounted to "collusion between the established unions, the management of SATS and the government in bringing about a controlled, racially based and a officially managed system of staff representation."

Food

South Africa's food and drinks industry employs 134,500 people, 85 per cent black and 15 per cent white. 60 per cent of the country's food crops are exported and many of the workers are considered as agricultural labourers and beyond the scope of legal union organisation. An important union in the Western Cape is the Food and Canning Workers Union which is a former SACTU affiliate. It survived during the 1970s and has developed strongly after the 1973 Durban strikes and now has 20,000 African and coloured members. It is one of the unaffiliated unions involved in the unity talks. FOSATU has two affiliated unions, the Sweet, Food and Allied Workers Union (SFAWU) with 10,000 members and in 1983 it accepted into membership the Natal Sugar Industry Employees Union which was founded in 1937 and has 1,000 members. Chris Dlamini, a Kellogs worker and SFAWU member is also president of FOSATU.

CUSA has a major affiliate, its Food, Beverage Workers Union with 10,000 members and many of the general and community unions also have pockets of workers in the multitude of plants and companies operating in the industry. The organisational fight has been uphill. 'Skates' Sikhakane, general secretary of the Food, Beverage Workers Union was arrested under the Internal Security Act early in 1984 when he went to a factory near Johannesburg to try to settle a dispute. The police also came to the homes of other union members who worked in the factory in order to question them.

Workers employed by the Natal dairy industry have also been victimised for trying to organise a union. At the Carmel Chocolate and Sweet Industries plant a union organiser was ordered off the premises and a worker was approached and asked if he belonged to the 'fucking shit of a union'. Another was offered a R30 increase if she resigned from the union. After the Christmas closure in 1983, management selectively rehired and refused to take back 25 workers who were SFAWU members.

However at a Natal hide and skin factory the SFAWU secured the reinstatement of workers who had gone on strike when five leading union members were fired. As so often in these reinstatement battles the case was on the point of being heard in court when the company agreed to a settlement and to take back the workers. Another organising success was when the FOSATU affiliate won recognition at the Congella Brewery in Durban. This brewery is owned by the Port Natal Administration Board. This may open the way to union recognition in other publicly-owned enterprises run by Administration Boards. In addition to securing the right to elect shop stewards and stop orders, the union won time off for union training.

The massive drought that has hit South Africa since 1981 has sent drink sales soaring and union organisation in drinks factories with it. In early 1984, 2,000 Coca Cola workers went on strike for higher wages and for access to details of the company pension fund. At the Suncrush bottling plant in Richards Bay, SFAWU members negotiated a wage increase of 18 per cent after an initial company offer of 10 per cent.

Insurance and Clerical

With South Africa's insurance companies now amongst the giant financial and commercial corporations of the country, the need for effective unionisation amongst the black clerical and administrative workers is long over-due. But it will be hard. The major dispute that developed in 1983 at Liberty Life, when the Insurance and Assurance Workers Union of South Africa (IAWUSA) tried to obtain recognition, shows the lengths to which the insurance companies will go to keep at bay unions for their black employees.

The union requested talks over recognition but were told that as it organised only African workers — IAWUSA is close to the black consciousness movement — the company, which claimed to follow a 'non-racial' policy would not agree to meaningful talks. IAWUSA's president, Joe Seoka, replied that Liberty Life's employment policy was far from 'non-racial'. The starting salary for a qualified African clerical worker was R320 a month while a white with the same qualifications started on R650 a month. Support for the union inside the company was shown when 100 workers came out on strike in support of higher wages. During the three-day strike, the strikers organised poster demonstratons outside the company head offices.

A second strike was called after the management still refused to talk to the union as the representatives of the workers. This time Liberty Life fired 93 workers and selectively re-hired. The union's response was to call upon Africans to withdraw their savings from Liberty Life companies.

The heartland of South African business and commerce — the Johannesburg headquarters of Anglo-American — was hit by a short strike by clerical workers in September 1983. This followed the dismissal of a photocopier operator, Walter Mnguno, who had 28 years service with Anglo-American. His offence was that he did not smile at some white staff! More than 100 members of the General and Allied Workers Union staged a strike, and demonstrated outside Anglo-American, until the management agreed to lift the dismissal notice.

They decided to try and organise a formal GAWU branch at Anglo-American. GAWU is one of the community-based unions. Many clerical workers are organised in the industrally based unions of FOSATU and CUSA as well as in general unions, but the office employees of banks, insurance companies and finance houses, (often a major source of white-collar union membership in other countries) remain, at least in terms of black clerical workers, to be organised in South Africa.

Metal and engineering

The metal manufacturing sector of South Africa is perhaps the key area for development for the emerging trade union movement. Of its 426,000 workers, 311,500 are black. They work in a large number of firms. The major metal union, the Metal and Allied Workers Union, MAWU, has 180 factories organised and has signed 122 recognition agreements. Organisation problems are immense. Seventy per cent of South Africa's manufacturing establishment have 50 or fewer employees. Although there have been rolling waves of recruitment, such as in the East Rand in 1982, the follow-up problems of organisation, developing shop steward structures and maintaining the union as a going concern in each local plant is difficult. MAWU's membership in 1983 was 36,000 yet it estimated that during the union's 10 years' existence it has probably recruited about 80,000 metalworkers. Finding the organisational capacity to keep each of those in continuing membership has been beyond the union's capabilities. Yet in comparison with some of the other black unions, MAWU is better organised, uses its 23 full-time officials more effectively and has an excellent record in negotiation and dispute handling.

Other important unions are the 24,000-strong Steel, Engineering and Allied Workers Union (SEAWU) and a smaller union, the Engineering and Allied Workers Union which broke away from the former. The general secretary of the SEAWU, Jane Hlongwane, is one of the longest serving black metal union leaders. Her union is affiliated to CUSA. The General and Allied Workers Union has been active recruiting steel and engineering workers in Transvaal and the General Workers Union also has a growing engineering worker membership in the Western Cape.

The metal unions face a determined opponent in South Africa's best organised employer's federation, the Steel, Engineering Industry Federation of South Africa (SEIFSA). SEIFSA has consistently resisted the advance of unions. Its tactics in the past have included refusing to negotiate with unregistered unions, insisting that all negotiations take place within the framework of the Industrial Council and advising companies not to sign plant level agreements. SEIFSA dominates the metal industry Industrial Council. This is a national council and sets wage rates for the entire industry. Since MAWU's entry into the Industrial Council the negotiations have taken a much harder direction.

Yet union action at the base has repeatedly overturned efforts by SEIFSA to control the metal unions. Scaw Metals is one of Anglo-American's most profitable companies; its 1983 profits were R66 million. In 1981, there was a strike by 3,000 workers at Scaws for higher wages. The chairman said he was a 'pillar of SEIFSA' and that he would not break SEIFSA's policy of not negotiating at plant level. The strike was broken when management called in the police to force workers back to the bantustans. The union kept organising, however, and by 1984 it had won the re-engagement of all the workers fired in the 1981 strike. MAWU shop stewards had also won consultation rights over the company's recruitment policy.

A major event in the metal industry was the rolling wave of strikes that hit the East Rand in 1982. MAWU rejected a low wage settlement offered by the Industrial Council. Workers turned to the union as it appeared to be the only organisation willing to fight back. In 1983, MAWU decided to join the Industrial Council providing it did not give up plant based bargaining as well. The economic recession meant that retrenchment became a major issue in 1983 and 1984. Companies have also used the excuse of economic problems and the need to slim down workforces to get rid of union militants. At the B and S Engineering factory at Brits in Transvaal, 900 workers were fired in September 1983 as the management sacked the entire workforce in order to remove the union's presence. Three hundred of the workers stayed together and held meetings every day as MAWU tried to get them reinstated; eventually they were successful and all 300 were taken back. At a carborundum factory in Port Elizabeth, MAWU went on strike to protect the jobs of seven workers. They were the firm's security guards whom the company wanted to replace with outside contractors. As a result of the strike the company agreed to keep the men on the payroll as production workers; the strike also revealed that the security guards had been consistently underpaid and they won R5,000 in back pay.

An important step forward was taken by the emerging unions when they won seats on the metal industries' pension fund. This has funds of more than R500 million and all black workers must belong. With the decision of the South African Boilermakers (which, despite its name, is a general metal union) to withdraw from TUCSA, the possibility of greater co-operation between metal unions is now on the cards. Another development was the setting of a South African co-ordinating council for metal unions under the auspices of the International Metalworkers Federation. Its full-time secretary, Brian Fredericks is a former official of the FOSATU auto union, NAAWU. In the early rounds of negotiations for the 1984 metal industry agreement, the white-run Boilermakers joined with MAWU and SEAWU in rejecting the SEIFSA offer — the first time there had been that kind of inter-union agreement on bargaining strategy.

Mining

South African's gold, metal, and coal mining industry lies at the centre of the country's wealth. After agriculture, mining is the most important source of employment. There are 550,000 black mine workers. Ninety-five per cent of these are migrants. They live in compounds, isolated from the townships and other industrial workers. The great mining strikes of 1922 and 1946 form an important and well-known part of South African history. Mineworkers were not organised in the 1950s and although there were strikes during the 1970s there was little effective organisation of black miners. Strikers were simply shunted back to the bantustans. There is a tightly supervised system of recruitment and it is easy both to blacklist known union activists and to engage strike-breakers from the many unemployed Africans.

By 1982, mineworkers had had enough. There was a strike by

70,000 in 13 gold mines. In one mine 120 workers sealed themselves in a tunnel. The main grievance was low wages and the poor living conditions in the compound. As Chapter 6 on health and safety shows, the dangerous working conditions in the mines are also a major concern. The 1982 strike was suppressed, leaving 10 dead and scores wounded and the usual expulsions to the bantustans.

In response to the strike several of the emerging unions tried to increase direct organisation of black mineworkers. The Council of Unions of South Africa sent one of the young experts from its legal department to begin an organising drive. His name is Cyril Ramophosa and in two years (1982-1984) the National Union of Mineworkers has become South Africa's biggest black union with 70,000 members. Born in 1952, Ramophosa was detained twice while a student. He was held for 11 months after his involvement in a rally in support of the Mozambique liberation movement, FRELIMO, in 1974 and then for six months in 1976 during the Soweto uprising. Ramophosa was questioned for four months during one of his detentions but says: "I feel sorry for the people who did that to me. They won't ever stop the tide of black people fighting for their rights."

As noted in the chapters on structure and organisation, and health and safety, the National Union of Mineworkers has concentrated on building up its shaft steward system and on increasing pressure on employers to improve safety standards. In 1982, the NUM was recognised by the Chamber of Mines. After the bitter strike of that year the Chamber, in the words of one of its officials, found it "easier to deal with recognised leaders of organised unions than to confront an angry mob". Ramophosa's calm, well-spoken manner belies a solid union organising ability. The NUM's 180-page shaft stewards' manual, which he was largely responsible for drafting, is an impressive document. The call for a protest stoppage over the Hlobane mining disaster, in which 68 miners were killed in September 1983, was widely followed. In the handful of mines that are not members of the Chamber of Mines, the NUM has fought hard for recognition. Seven hundred mineworkers went on strike at an open-cast coalmine near Witbank. The mine's management wanted shop stewards to be elected according to procedures laid down by the company. The strike changed their mind and they agreed to recognise the NUM's shop steward committee.

Other unions are also trying to organise black mineworkers in various parts of the country. MAWU has one organiser working on recruiting miners and there is also the Black Allied Miners Construction Workers Union which is closely linked to AZAPO, the Azania People's Organisation. In Kimberley, at the De Beers diamond mines, the Federated Mining Union, which is an offshoot of the South African Boilermakers Society is successfully organising black workers. There is also a very powerful, all-white union in the industry — the Mine Workers Union. This union went on strike in 1979 to protect jobs reserved for whites only. The strike was crushed but the union has allied itself with extreme, right-wing break-away elements in the Nationalist Party, unhappy at what they consider to be too many concessions made to blacks by the government. The mining industry still has the last legal job reservation and no black can obtain the 'blaster's certificate' which permits promotion into the ranks of skilled mineworkers. The white MWU has said it will take any action to defend its members' privileged position.

Municipal workers

Organising black municipal workers has proved extremely difficult. This section of workers has suffered two major blows in the 1980s. Firstly, the crushing of the 1980 Johannesburg municipal workers' strike. Then, in 1982, the death in a car accident of Joseph Mavi, president of the Black Municipal Workers Union, removed one of the most effective black union leaders in South Africa. The 1980 strike was over a recognition and a claim by electricians for an increase in the minimum wage of R33 per week. It spread quickly and within days 15,000 workers were on strike. Streets were not cleaned and garbage left uncollected. The strike was broken by the police. They asked workers at gunpoint if they would return to work or if they wanted to be expelled to the bantustans. One thousand four hundred workers were dismissed and told to pack their belongings and return to their bantustans. Mavi, who had earlier organised his fellow bus drivers and won better wages for them, had formed the Black Municipal Workers Union only a short time before the strike. The Johannesburg City Council refused to negotiate with him; instead he was arrested and kept in solitary confinement. Ater his release in 1981, Mavi tried to get the union off the ground again, but he was detained for two months in the middle of 1981 after speaking at a meeting. His death in an accident in June 1982 was a cruel blow to the Johannesburg municipal workers.

The South African Black Municipal and Allied Workers Union (SABMAWU) is affiliated to CUSA and has 20,000 members. It has patiently tried to expand its organisation, adopting a more concilatory approach than the Mavi tradition. Attempts to get recognition agreements with the Rand Water Board have been brushed aside. The FOSATU affiliated Transport and General

Workers Union staged a march though the centre of a Durban suburb and a sit-down in front of the civic centre by 200 municipal workers calling for higher pay and union recognition. The town clerk agreed to call a meeting of the council to discuss an interim recognition agreement. This public, peaceful protest surprised white shoppers. Like other public employees, municipal workers face different, perhaps greater difficulties than private sector workers but the drive for organisation is there. At the 1983 annual congress of the Municipal and General Workers Union of South Africa (MGWUSA) workers presented a long list of complaints, including the newly introduced practice of giving two weeks' unpaid leave, which means that a migrant worker cannot build up consecutive employment time in order to qualify as a permanent resident in Johannesburg. Workers also called for a wage increase and condemned the city council for its support of a management controlled union for black workers. They decided to elect a shop stewards' committee to press these demands. In Cape Town, the Cape Town Municipal Workers Association has become more active and participated with other Cape unions in the talks around forming a united federation of independent unions.

Print and paper

The main black union for print workers is the Media Workers Association of South Africa (MWASA). Of its 2,000 members, about 1,800 work in newspapers as drivers, clerks and in typographical departments, while the remaining 200 are journalists. Most of South Africa's best-known black journalists, like Joe Tholoe and Zwelakhe Sisulu, son of the imprisoned ANC leader, Walter Sisulu, are MWASA members. Indeed, journalists occupy nearly all the leadership positions in the Transvaal, Western Cape and Natal branches.

MWASA began life as the Writers Association of South Africa which was set up in 1977 after the Union of Black Journalists was banned. The decision to open up the union to all media workers has increased its membership but brought new problems. Although MWASA was able to develop solidarity action by its Johannesburg members in 1980 in support of striking Cape Town *Argus* workers, a strike by MWASA printers on the Johannesburg *Star* in 1982 was crushed and 209 printers lost their jobs. Most MWASA journalists work on black newspapers like the *Sowetan* or the *City Press* or for the black supplements of the English language newspapers and their capacity for effective solidarity action with printers is limited.

The founders of MWASA were closely linked to the black consciousness movement. There is a white journalists' union, the

South African Society of Journalists (SASJ) which from the middle 1970s onwards has taken a radical and, by South African standards, a brave stand, in attacking the effects of apartheid on journalism and in criticising the limited career opportunities open to black journalists. The SASJ de-registered itself in order to open its ranks to black journalists, the only white union to have thus acted. The black journalists however felt that as a minority in the SASJ they would have no influence and, following the black consciousness line, argued that the differences between whites and blacks were so great that to come together in a trade union dealing with workplace matters was pointless.

The problems of a blacks only policy, and the dominant role of journalists in MWASA, came to a head late in 1983 and by the middle of 1984, the union had split in two. The row started when the Cape Town MWASA members decided to affiliate to the United Democratic Front. They also proposed to change the union's constitution to make it non-racial. This would have had little practical effect as MWASA's only possible area of expansion is among black workers. However the Transvaal leaders of MWASA reacted strongly against both proposals. Here one enters difficult areas of speculation about motives, as the Johannesburg black journalists contain both strong black consciousness oriented people, as well as those linked to the ANC non-racial traditions. In Cape Town MWASA has a higher proportion of non-journalists in its membership by comparison with Johannesburg. A stormy congress failed to resolve these problems and though attempts at conciliation were made during the first months of 1984 these came to nothing.

A continually expanding union can take this kind of problem in its stride but MWASA's main obstacle to growth in the newspaper industry has been the powerful TUCSA union, the 43,000-strong South African Typographical Union (SATU). This is a long established, white-run craft union that has the well-policed and enforced closed shop often found in print industries. It thus automatically pulls into membership black workers and its medical, insurance and retirement schemes provide attractive benefits that MWASA could not hope to match.

In the paper and packaging industry, on the other hand, the FOSATU affiliated Paper, Wood and Allied Workers Union (PWAWU) has made considerable progress. In several firms ballots of all the workers have shown massive majorities for PWAWU. At Kohler Corrugated, for example, a ballot of 288 workers in July 1983 had 273 voting to be represented by PWAWU. Firms are being forced to grant partial exemptions to SATU's closed shop in the face of workers' determination to be represented by a union of their own choice. The union has also taken strike action to secure recognition. Three hundred and fifty workers went on strike for a week at the Premier Paper Mill after management only gave wage increases to a selected 48 workers. The company also cancelled the recognition agreement but the resulting strike made them change their minds and come to terms with the union.

There are about 29,000 black workers in the South African paper industry and many of them work in small companies with fewer than 100 employees. A dispute at the Johannesburg plastic bag manufacturer, Transpoly, in March 1984, which employed only 85 workers, showed PWAWU's determination to organise smaller firms, where working conditions — including an alleged working week of 84 hours at Transpoly — are often extremely bad. Workers went on strike and all of them were dismissed. The company called in the police who arrested a PWAWU organiser. The union's response was to contact workers in firms that use Transpoly's products and ask them to black them. This tactic plus the threat of legal action changed the company's mind and they reinstated half the fired workers and paid the other R35,000 as compensation. PWAWU said it hoped the case would serve "as a warning to other companies with similar abysmal labour practices".

Retail

The only union operating with real effect in organising retail workers is the Commercial, Catering and Allied Workers Union of South Africa (CCAWUSA). It has won recognition agreements with major South African chain stores including OK Bazaars, Pick'n Pay and Woolworths. Founded in 1975, it was lucky to have as an advisor Morris Kagan, a veteran socialist from Latvia and one of the best-known trade union organisers in South Africa. He was a former president of the National Union of Distributive Workers and worked with SACTU's African Commercial Workers' Union until it was crushed in the repression of the early 1960s. CCAWUSA's energetic general secretary, Emma Mashinini, has also used a wide range of tactics to spread the union's strength. The Union is regularly involved in strikes and is spreading its organisation into hotels. Strikes by hotel workers have hit the giant Southern Sun chain and Johannesburg's top hotel, the Carlton.

One of the most interesting aspects of CCAWUSA's work is the variety of mechanisms the union deploys to achieve its ends. During the 1983 wage negotiations with OK Bazaars, the union used the Conciliation Board machinery laid down in the Labour Relations Act. A company offer of a R20 a month was pushed up to R35 a month after three conciliation board hearings. The union also broke new ground in using outside arbitrators to settle a case over a sacked worker. He was fired by the wholesalers Makro after allegations of assault and insubordination. The union went through the disputes procedure laid down in the agreement but failed to win the worker's reinstatement. Two strikes also failed to move the company. Finally, the union suggested appointing two outside arbitrators — one to be chosen by CCAWUSA, the other by Makro — and they would make a binding decision. As it happened their decision was in favour of the worker, but this was the first time that a union had succeeded in persuading a company to allow such outside arbitration.

CCAWUSA has been one of the pioneering unions in getting maternity agreements with companies. It is also one of the few non-racial unions which has seen common action undertaken by black and white workers. In October 1983, management at one of the Germiston branches of Checkers demoted a woman worker. There was also a general discontent about the store manager's attitude to the workforce. Workers went on strike and secured the woman's reinstatement and extracted an apology from the store manager. What was interesting was that the demoted woman was white and both black and white workers went on strike. The union has also used threats of boycotts against stores, though with limited success.

Textile and clothing

240,000 black workers are employed in this sector, and the clothing industry alone is South Africa's fifth largest employer. There is a rich history of militant trade union organisation and the Garment Workers Union led by Solly Sachs, a communist, was one of the most successful unions in the 1930s and 1940s. Textile workers also spearheaded the 1973 Durban strikes. There are four textile and garment unions affiliated to TUCSA and the history of organisation in the industry is one of great inter-union rivalry with companies actively supporting TUCSA unions against the claims of FOSATU's National Union of Textile Workers (NUTW) and CUSA's Transvaal Textile Workers' Union.

Outside the metal industry, this sector has seen the highest level of strike activity by the emerging trade union movement. February 1984, for example, saw three major strikes over pay in Pinetown, near Durban. Four hundred workers went on strike for 10 days at SA Fabrics, a subsidiary of the British Courtaulds group. The company had offered an increase of 4 per cent, against the workers' claim for 10 per cent. In a secret ballot 91 per cent of the workers voted to go on strike. At Smith and Nephew, 600 workers went on strike for higher wages, while at the Ninian and Lester factory 80 shift. workers struck to have an unpopular shift system abolished. When the company fired them the entire workforce came out in support. The shift system was scrapped. The union all these workers belonged to, the National Union of Textile Workers, broke new ground the year before when it organised the first ever legal strike by black workers in South Africa.

The union patiently worked its way through the lengthy procedures of the Labour Relations Act, which are usually ignored as workers respond quickly to a sense of grievance by taking immediate strike action. The more than 400 workers were willing to wait and follow the union's strategy of seeking to go on strike legally. It was worth it because after the nine-day strike the Natal Thread Company not only came up with a 15 per cent an hour wage increase (plus back pay), they also agreed to a clause in the settlement agreement which stated that in the event of future strikes they would either dismiss all strikers or none of them. This was an important development in South African collective bargaining as the selective re-hiring of strikers is a commonly used weapon enabling managements to weed out strike leaders and union activists.

Although the NUTW has only 18,000 members its support is growing. The main obstacle is the set of closed shop agreements covering black workers which companies have signed with TUCSA unions in order to keep the NUTW at bay. It was this problem that led the NUTW to reverse its policy of non-recognition of Industrial Councils, and seek instead, to join them in order to gain access to workers covered by Industrial Council closed shop agreements. The NUTW joined the Transvaal knitting industry Industrial Council while preserving its right to continue plant level bargaining where it deemed it necessary.

Two important steps in breaking the TUCSA domination of the Natal garment industry were taken early in 1984. At the multi-nationally owned James North Africa factory, the management agreed to a ballot of workers to see which union they wished to represent them. Eighty-one point four per cent voted in favour of the NUTW. Another step forward was when the union secured a court judgement permitting it to take the Frame Group of companies to the Industrial Court over the Frame Group's persistent refusal to recognise or negotiate with the NUTW. The Frame Group is South Africa's largest textile employer, with over 4,000 employees at one Durban plant alone. Although the NUTW has signed up many Frame workers, the company has refused to permit ballots to see which union workers preferred. Instead it has always supported the different TUCSA textile unions. One of the TUCSA unions, the Textile Workers Industrial Union, has turned to violence to stop the NUTW recruiting Frame workers. An NUTW organiser, Jabulani Gwala and two women NUTW members were attacked by TWIU members while they were leafleting outside a Frame factory near Durban. In February 1984, another worker had his arm broken while trying to recruit for the NUTW.

Transport

The major transport employer in South Africa, the South African Transport Services (SATS), which has 150,000 african employees is off-limits to the emerging trade unions. As noted in the section on dock workers, attempts to organise have been crushed. In 1983, the government passed the Conditions of Employment (South African Services Act) which legaly entrenched SATS's refusal to deal with the independent unions. The act allows only staff associations recognised by the Minister of Transport to function with the conciliation machinery which is controlled, in any case, by SATS. Employees are forbidden from initiating or taking part in strike action. The Act also reverts to forms of disguised job reservation. All workers who are not citizens of South Africa are to be denied permanent or temporary appointments and instead will be treated as 'casual' workers. This will affect about 50,000 SATS workers who come from bantustans and thus considered as 'foreigners' by the South African government. It will severely limit promotion and training possibilities though these are the least advanced of any South African industry in any case. In 1982, South African Railways indentured 1,647 apprentices. Only seven were black.

If SATS is, for the time being, a no-go area, the emerging unions are making headway organising in the private transport undertakings and with some municipal bus companies. The two main unions are FOSATU's Transport and General Workers Union (TGWU) which has 9,000 members and CUSA's Transport and Allied Workers Union (TAWU), also with 9,000 members.

Some headway has been made with PUTCO, South Africa's biggest private bus company. Bus companies are defined in legislation as 'essential services' so unions have to go through mediation and arbitration procedures. The TGWU has recently made PUTCO go to arbitration following unsatisfactory negotiations. There has been more success with municipal bus companies. As noted at the beginning of this book a strike by Durban bus drivers in March 1984, won union recognition for the TGWU. In fact, nearly all the bus companies in the Natal region have been organised. The TGWU has also been moving into the private freight transport area. A recognition agreement signed with

Freight Air and Freight Services Forwarding in August 1983 was the first agreement by an independent union and a goods transport company.

Chapter 9

Black Unions and the Search for Unity

Although the growth of the independent unions has been swift and substantial, many obstacles confront them. None is potentially more dangerous than the divisions that have plagued the unions since their emergence. At first these divisions had little impact on the day-to-day functioning of the unions. As we have seen, each pursued its own path separated from the others by both space and a sea of unorganised labour. Unions that emerged in Cape Town had little need to consult labour organisers in Johannesburg, nearly 1,000 miles away. Each union centre developed its own character and form of organisation reflecting the political and geographic environment in which they found themselves. Even when unions organised subsidiaries of the same firm, they seldom felt constrained to co-operate with unions at such distances. In addition the political divisions that exist in the black working class were reflected in the unions. Thus in Natal the Zulu-based organisation Inkatha was a factor to be reckoned with. In the Eastern Cape the strong ANC tradition helped shape the unions along non-racial lines. And in the Witwatersrand black consciousness had a major influence in the early 1970s.

Yet as the unions developed, the need to co-operate became ever more apparent. Firstly there were cases in which union solidarity amongst unions organising the same firm in different areas would be obviously beneficial. Then, as the unions expanded their membership, the ocean of unorganised labour was gradually reduced, and the potential for inter-union rivalry grew. Although there were still vast numbers of unorganised workers, many were in sectors of the economy that were exceedingly difficult to organise — such as agriculture or mining. Finally there was the impetus provided by the state. In a negative way the state gave the unions the greatest rationale for unity. On the one hand the government issued a series of reports — Wiehahn and Riekerts — that were designed to govern the behaviour of unions. A response to these had to be given, and a unified response would be so much more powerful than a disparate series of stands. On the other hand, the state's repeated crackdowns on union leaders and members tended to weld the union movement together, despite their differences. In reality the death of Neil Aggett and the wave of repression launched by the Ciskei authorities probably did more than anything else to bring the unions together.

First unity summit

Although preliminary discussions about unity had been going on since late 1979, the first unity summit was held on 8 August 1981. On that day over 100 representatives of 29 independent unions met at Langa in Cape Town. All the major unions were represented, including FOSATU, CUSA, SAAWU and the Cape Unions. The meeting's primary purpose was to formulate a united response to the government's labour legislation. However, resolutions on several other issues were discussed and agreed. The resolutions covered the boycotting of Industrial Councils; union harassment by the Ciskei authorities; detentions and solidarity action. The unions agreed to co-operate with each other in resisting the state, and decided to establish ad hoc solidarity committees to encourage inter-union co-operation in each region. It was agreed that the committees would "... discuss and initiate solidarity action arising out of our co-operation". Sadly, the promise of the first historic meeting in Langa gave way to a series of ever more divided meetings, in which the fractious tendencies within the union movement were given full reign.

The second meeting was scheduled to take place in November 1981, but finally got under way over the weekend of 24 and 25 April 1982. The setting was Wilgespruit in the Transvaal. The meeting took place against a background of detentions — that hit GAWU, SAAWU and FCWU in particular — and the very limited success achieved by the solidarity committees. Although the meeting was felt to make some progress, with a spirit of unity at the gathering, it also saw the kind of behaviour that was to dog future meetings. MACWUSA argued that it would have no truck with any union that registered with, or was a member of, the Industrial Councils, and walked out of the meeting, calling on other unregistered unions to do likewise. The meeting concluded that more detailed discussions on unity were needed.

The third unity meeting took place in Port Elizabeth on 3, 4 July that year. The meeting was the most divisive to date, with the emergence of the factions that still divide the movement today. The only real point of agreement was on the broad principle of workers' control over the unions. Even this general commitment to democracy was qualified by the insistence of CUSA that workers' control should mean black workers control. Even this highly qualified unity would in all probability have dissolved if its practical consequences had been examined.

The meeting was divided into broadly two camps. On the one side were the hardliners, which included SAAWU, BMWU, GAWU, OVGWU, MACWUSA, GWUSA. These unions took their stand on what they felt were non-negotiable principles. These principles should form the basis of a new federation and were: non-registration with the state's Industrial Councils; federation policies binding on affiliates; non-racialism; workers' control; participation in community issues; rejection of reactionary bodies nationally and internationally. They insisted that the resolutions adopted at the first meeting in Langa should form the basis of any discussions concerning unity.

Disagreement over registration

Ranged against the hardliners were a more disparate grouping of more pragmatic unions, including FOSATU, CUSA, GWU and FCWU. All but the GWU had unions that were members of the Industrial Councils and/or were registered. Certainly these unions, which had by far the largest membership, were not prepared to be lectured to by the seven and were not going to be told that certain demands were non-negotiable. Nonetheless, the pragmatists did have their differences. FOSATU called for a disciplined unity, in which all member organisations would be bound by the decisions of the proposed federation — something that already took place in FOSATU. The GWU and CUSA, again reflecting their own experiences, argued for a loose federation, with a high degree of autonomy for component unions. In the event the arguments were academic, since the meeting collapsed with many bitter recriminations.

A series of highly critical articles appeared in the unions' respective newspapers attacking the positions adopted by the contesting parties. In December 1982 the General Workers Union published an attack on the hardliners which accused one of its members — MACWUSA — of scabbing during a recent industrial dispute. It went on to argue that the Langa resolutions could not be binding on future action, and could not be a precondition to unity. The article concluded by calling for the formation of a loose federation in which the views of each affiliate would be respected, and no-one would have the ability to dictate policy to anyone else.

This was followed by two articles that appeared in March 1983, arguing from two very different perspectives. The Orange Vaal General Workers Union argued, in a document that they prepared in anticipation of the unity meeting scheduled for April that year, that the basis for unity was amongst the workers themselves. As one of their headings suggested — who has been divided, workers or leadership? They returned to the agreement reached in Langa, which had made provision for the establishment of solidarity action committees, which would bring together workers in a given location irrespective of the union to which they belonged. They said that the reason for the failure of such committees was that they had not been seriously implemented. They refused to believe that workers in any location were not interested in forging such links, and pointed to a number of instances which they believed showed that workers were already in practice giving each other this kind of support. Local meetings should be convened at which solidarity action committees would be elected at mass meetings. The committees would, in effect take over the functions previously undertaken by the unions, since they would be capable of binding all workers represented at the meetings, to a particular course of action. Not surprisingly this formula received little support from those workers and unions that had spent many hard years building their union structures as effective forms of organisation.

The second proposal came in the form of an editorial in *FOSATU Workers' News*. The March issue set out to explain to workers the basis upon which the Federation would participate in the April meeting. FOSATU argued that what was required for a successful meeting was a "unity of purpose and political direction", since without a common perspective there would be wide differences which would prevent "common worker action". The other prerequisite for a successful meeting was pragmatism. The Federation professed itself to be ready to debate and compromise on all its positions, except this commitment to workers' control of union affairs and non-racialism. The Editorial concluded by warning that "all talk and no action is a dangerous game".

In the event the warning went unheeded. Although the meeting on 9, 10 April 1983 did agree to set up a steering committee representing 14 of the 29 unions that attended the meeting, charged with finding the most appropriate structure for a new federation (the remainder agreed to the idea of a federation, but felt constrained to seek a mandate before joining the steering committee), little else was forthcoming. The meeting was deeply split on the best way forward. The split took place along familiar lines. On the one side SAAWU, OVGWU, GAWU and MACWUSA — on this issue joined by CUSA — argued that the way forward was by means of solidarity action committees. On the other hand were the FCWU, GWU and FOSATU, which argued that the committees had been tried and had failed. They said that the problem was that the committees were mainly attended by officials and had generally been characterised by rivalry and disagreement. Together with CCAWUSA, these unions declared in favour of a federation. The CTMWA supported their position, but argued that a federation should be supplemented by solidarity action committees. During the course of the first day the SAAWU came round to agreeing that a federation might be desirable, and the second day was then spent discussing existing union structures.

Essentially the reason why the committees were attractive to the regional or general unions was because it would allow them to expand beyond their regional bases, and secondly, because it would allow them to continue without being fractured into their industrial components, ultimately to be absorbed into the larger, existing industrial unions. The industrial unions, on the other hand, were not prepared to lose their national status, a status which had allowed them to unionise different plants in the same company.

When the steering committee met in Cape Town on 2, 3 July 1983 some of the unions that had expressed their reservations about the steering committee were present, evidently having been given a mandate by their membership to attend. And the meeting proved to be one of the most fruitful that the movement had held since it had begun seeking unity two years earlier. The two opposing blocs of unions were not in evidence, and unions voted for and against points according to their convictions. Most of the time was devoted to discussing the future structure of the federation, with some unions arguing for a complex structure, while others felt that the federation should be kept simple. Divisions did emerge over two issues, namely on the future role and powers of union officials, and external funding. Some of the unions felt that officials should have voting rights where they had a clear mandate, while others felt that voting should only be by worker delegates. On funding some felt that the federation should be wholly dependent upon the resources that its membership could provide, while others argued that outside assistance was essential to the viability of the organisation.

Divisions continue

But if the April meeting was productive, the next meeting which was held in Johannesburg on 8, 9 October 1983 was as divisive as ever. For the July meeting had agreed that all unions would submit information on the areas in which they were organising and their proposals for the new federation. However the hardline unions failed to live up to their commitment. This soured the meeting and the atmosphere degenerated further when a number of unions insisted that demarcation should be discussed as a matter of urgency. There then followed a bitter argument between GWU and CCAWUSA on the one hand and SAAWU on the other with the two accusing SAAWU of poaching their members and disrupting

organising activities. Arising from the discussions, FOSATU
proposed that all unions should accept a commitment to the
principle of 'one union, one industry', but failed to win acceptance
at the meeting.

Agreement was hindered by the fact that the hardliners had
failed to provide adequate information concerning their
operations, and they came under pressure from the rest of the
meeting to provide the information by the following day, or
withdraw from the meeting. On the ninth the hardliners gave some
general information about the sectors and areas in which they were
organising, but the unevenness of the information made
comparisons difficult. As a result little practical was achieved. It
was agreed that a co-ordinating committee should be formed
comprising two delegates from each union to discuss the problem
of demarcation. In reality there was little hope of an accord, since
for the general unions to agree to clear lines of demarcation would
be to submit to their own dismemberment by the industrial unions.
Only general unions like the GWU, which had previously begun to
specialise into areas such as the docks, could hope to survive once
genuine demarcation took place.

Many of the unions found the October meeting deeply
depressing, for it had become evident that there was not likely to be
the possibility of a federation that included all the unions that had
been involved in the discussions from the start. In October the
FOSATU Central Committee, for example, decided that bilateral
negotiations should begin with like-minded unions, and a
delegation was selected, instructed to meet with the other more
pragmatic unions, such as FCWU, CUSA, CTMWA, GWU and
CCAWUSA. All of these unions agreed that there appeared little
hope of unity with the hardliners, but one last meeting should be
held to try to resolve the differences.

The meeting was held in Johannesburg on 3, 4 March 1984. It
opened with a proposal by the FCWU that the meeting could only
proceed if there could be clarity on who was ready to join a
federation. The union proposed that in order for a union to be
ready for unity it would have to satisfy the following three
conditions:

1. The union must have taken a clear decision with no conditions
   that it is prepared to join a new federation.
2. Federations must have decided to disband in order to form a
   new federation.
3. General unions must be in the process of forming industrially
   demarcated unions or of confining their activities to certain
   clearly defined industries. Those unions that were not able to
   meet the criteria should be offered observer status in the talks

until such time as they could meet the criteria, at which time they would rejoin the talks as full participants. This position was accepted by CCAWUSA, CTMWA, CUSA, FOSATU and GWU. The hardliners, namely SAAWU, GAWU and MCWUSA all raised objections. SAAWU asked for a postponement, and after the lunch break the three unions were informed that they should either accept observer status or leave the meeting. Under protest the unions left, leaving those unions that had already achieved a great deal of unity to look at the details of the federation that they were now determined to set up.

Since that decisive meeting there has been rapid progress towards the formation of a federation that will encompass the vast majority of all the non-racial unions in the country.

Chapter 10

Unions, Politics and the Liberation Movement

The repression of the early '60s removed the South African Congress of Trade Unions's (SACTU) leadership from South Africa. Although never officially banned, its leadership was decimated by arrests, detentions and bannings (see Chapter 2). Five SACTU activists died in detention. Those that survived either decided to lay low, or went into exile. The capacity to organise workers in unions inside South Africa had been destroyed. In the years that followed, the SACTU leadership, in conjunction with the rest of the Congress movement, used the international arena to expose the suppression of trade union rights in South Africa as part of its condemnation of apartheid. SACTU claimed to have an underground network inside South Africa, but one can only speculate about its role. By any analysis the years between 1964 and 1973 were ones of industrial quietude.

It was the 'Durban' strikes and the events that preceded them in 1972/73 that sparked off a renewal of trade union activity amongst black workers. Some of the activists of the '70s had been active a decade earlier, and memory of SACTU's work remained. One former SACTU union was still in existence — the Food and Canning Workers Union — but it was a ghost of its former self, and to all intents and purposes had to be built anew. So for the majority of workers drawn into the unions in the '70s the organisations were a new phenomenon.

As the unions grew in membership and organisational competence in the '70s and early '80s SACTU was faced with something of a dilemma. In their literature and public statements the organisation had portrayed the apartheid state as fascist. Any form of genuine trade union activity would be inimicable to such a state. The idea that unionisation could take hold in such arid soil seemed to be little more than wishful thinking.

SACTU's analysis

Yet take hold it did. Gradually, and despite intense repression, black union membership grew to its present level of around 500,000. Firmly rooted in the militancy of the black working class, the movement has carved an increasingly significant place for itself in the South African political economy. Yet despite this impressive performance. SACTU has remained essentially unconvinced that anything but sham unionisation could take place. In a paper published in June 1977 John Gaetsewe, General Secretary of SACTU put the case with considerable clarity.

"What then is the role of open, legal trade unions for African workers?

"Organisation on all possible levels is vital in the development of the fighting strength of the workers, to meet the great challenges which lie ahead. In the day-to-day battles for the higher wages, better working conditions and trade union rights, the organisation and consciousness of the workers has advanced. For this reason, it has always been the policy of the South African Congress of Trade Unions (SACTU) to encourage and further the struggle for open trade unions in South Africa, and for trade union recognition.

"At the same time, SACTU recognises that there are ultimately only two options open to legal African trade unions: either to advance, taking up political as well as economic questions, and eventually being crushed or driven underground; or for the leadership to become co-opted and the unions emasculated — tools in the hands of the employers and registered unions . . . Repression of trade union activity means that in the long term, meaningful advances can only be made on an underground basis."

While such an attitude may have been correct in the early '70s, the continued growth and vitality of the movement increasingly brought it into question. Yet as late as 1982 a similar position was being adopted. In a major restatement of its position in June 1982, entitled 'SACTU's Present Role', the organisation spoke on the one hand of the "open trade union movement becoming a powerful force". And on the other hand it reiterated the line that repression would in the end win out.

"SACTU was forced underground. And there is nothing to suggest that the apartheid regime will ever tolerate a strong, progressive and open trade union movement for very long. It would be a mistake to act on this basis."

In the statement SACTU was portrayed as fulfilling three functions. First it claimed to be active in those sectors closed to the 'open' unions, such as the mines, the farms and the bantustans. The claim to be active on the mines was more than a little ironic, given SACTU's conspicuous failure to make any headway on the mines during its period of open trade union activity in the 1950s. The second claim was that it "sows the seeds for open trade unions to emerge, also creating a second level of leadership and continuously drawing new people into the trade union movement". Finally it acted at an international level to win support for, and channel funds to, the open unions in their struggle for survival.

A real tension permeates this analysis. If it is a mistake to act in the belief that the unions could play an effective role in the long run, why seek to succour, protect and strengthen the very organisations that are doomed to be crushed? Is it simply that workers must pass through unionisation as a step to some higher plane? Was not the organisation misleading workers in channelling them into unions that are pre-ordained to fail? The statement is unclear on all these questions, balancing a strange fatalism with a desire to encourage and assist.

In a sense these contradictions arise from the portrayal of the South African state as 'fascist'. While no-one is under any illusion about the repressive and authoritarian nature of the apartheid regime given the long list of deaths in detention, banishments, bannings and forced removals, it is simply misleading to label it fascist. It could be argued that those who employ such terminology do so as a form of abuse, or perhaps to convey to a European audience the severity of conditions under which the mass of the people in South Africa have to live. But such arguments are undermined by the analysis that SACTU employs. For it is from the analysis that South Africa is a fascist state that the belief arises that 'there is nothing to suggest that the apartheid regime will ever tolerate a strong, progressive and open trade union movement for very long'.

The emphasis of the statement is clear: the state is portrayed as all powerful and the opposition as essentially weak and reactive. In this analysis only the underground struggle stands any chance of success. It is an analysis that serves a real function — to warn off the international labour movement from links with the unions, since these are at best temporary phenomena. Its real purpose is to attempt to suggest that SACTU remains the only legitimate focus for workers' struggles in South Africa. The hope is that by maintaining this illusion all assistance to the unions in South Africa will be channelled via SACTU, and that SACTU will thereby maintain a hold over the open unions inside South Africa. It is in the end a strategy aimed at controlling the movement that its purports to assist.

The problems that SACTU faced were not lessened by the establishment in 1979 of the Federation of South African Trade Unions (FOSATU) and the Council of Unions of South Africa (CUSA) in 1980. For the first time since the 1960s there existed in South Africa trade union centres that could legitimately speak on behalf of the workers of South Africa. Unlike the Trade Union Council of South Africa (TUCSA), FOSATU and CUSA could not be dismissed as tools of the South African state. Yet their existence raised implicitly questions about the future of SACTU.

Independent unions develop links abroad

This uneasy relationship was not assisted when the independent unions began to extend their influence abroad. Hitherto the international scene had been the exclusive preserve of SACTU, and the organisation reacted sharply when this monopoly was challenged. The British Trade Union-SACTU liaison group stated in 1977 that the apartheid regime was resorting to sending abroad moderate trade unionists to 'explain' the position. 'They are easily distinguished by the fact that they hold South African passports, a commodity which under Apartheid rules is not available to any South African citizen who wishes to travel abroad to promote the interests of oppressed workers.'

Such an accusation could be applied with considerable justification to some of the emissaries sent abroad by organisations such as TUCSA, whose chief purpose was to denounce SACTU. Unfortunately the statement was bandied about without distinction, and a number of representatives of the independent, non-racial unions found themselves regarded with less than fraternal friendship. Although SACTU never formally attacked the independent unions, dark hints about their 'true' role were dropped on more than one occasion.

FOSATU, for its part, was both taken aback and more than a little disturbed by the hostility that it encountered. The concern was heightened when it became clear that the tensions between SACTU and the independent unions was being used as a vehicle for left-right battles within the international trade union movement. FOSATU was not prepared to be used as a vehicle to attack SACTU, which some on the right of the international trade union movement saw as a communist front.

At this time two further disputes complicated the scene. The first was a dispute within SACTU London headquarters concerning its policy and direction. The second was a conflict within the British Anti-Apartheid Movement over relations with the independent unions.

Divisions inside SACTU

The dispute within SACTU, which had been simmering for some time, erupted in July 1979 with the dismissal of the editor of SACTU's paper, *Workers' Unity,* and the members of the London-based Technical Sub-Committee after a period in which the work of *Workers' Unity* became 'bogged down in conflict which reflected serious political differences on what the role and tasks of SACTU were' as the dismissed editor put it. The differences were

summarised in 1979 by the dismissed members of SACTU as
follows:

● That the lack of urgency and commitment to the tasks of building
SACTU at home (and with it, developing the paper) was a result of a lack
of political clarity within the organisation and among the leadership of the
character and tasks of the South African revolution.

● That the cornerstone of SACTU's approach to the revolution must be
the recognition that neither economic gains, nor national liberation, nor
democracy can be secured for the black workers on the basis of capitalism,
but only through an uninterrupted struggle to overthrow capitalism and
begin the building of socialism.

● That the black working class is the only social force capable of leading
this revolutionary struggle in the interests of all the oppressed, and, to
undertake this task, must be organised first and foremost as workers.

● That the workers must be mobilised with the aim, at the decisive point,
of defeating the armed force of the state with the revolutionary armed force
of the mass movement.

● That the path to this goal lies in giving clear priority to building organs of
mass struggle, so that at every point the politics of the mass struggle
exercise command over the gun and the bomb."

Not surprisingly, the SACTU leadership reacted angrily to this
criticism. In particular they were stung by the charge of inactivity in
South Africa and what the dissidents referred to as 'isolation from
the workers' movement in South Africa'. The criticism was seen as
an attack on the strategy adopted by the Congress Alliance over a
number of years, including the theory of a two-stage revolution
(first bourgeois democratic and then socialist) and the consequent
need to build the broadest coalition of forces to oppose the
apartheid state.

The criticism drew a sharp reply from an anonymous 'reader' in
African Communist, the theoretical journal of the South African
Communist Party, in its third quarter issue of 1980. The strategy of
the dissidents was attacked as both economistic and workerist. It
was incorrect because it saw the liberation struggle solely in terms
of the working class, ignoring the role of other layers or classes of
the oppressed. As the author put it, such an analysis results in ". . .
the total collapse of the entire political and armed struggle of the
popular masses into the trade union movement and the
abandonment of any conception of an alliance in the revolutionary
struggle between the working class and the 'rural poor' together,
under the appropriate conditions, with the petty bourgeoisie.
Worse still, such an analysis poses a threat to the Congress Alliance
itself, for it elevates the trade union movement to a general political
and revolutionary role. This is to seek to usurp the place and

function of the ANC and its allies: it leads . . . to the substitution
of SACTU for other political organisations.''

Whatever the merits of the respective positions the editor of the
paper remained dismissed and the technical Committee remained
disbanded. Together with a group of like-minded people they went
off to form the South African Labour Education Project,
publishing *Inqaba Ya Basebenzi,* which they referred to as the
*Journal of the Marxist Workers' Tendency of the African National
Congress.* Close to the Trotskyist Militant Tendency within the
British Labour Party, the dissidents build links with the British
labour movement, while also engaging in educational activities in
Germany and the Netherlands.

Anti-apartheid and fraternal visits

The debate within the British Anti-Apartheid Movement concerned
relations between the union movement in Britain and the
independent unions in South Africa. The debate, which led to
heated exchanges at the Anti-Apartheid AGMs in 1981 and 1982,
centred on whether relations with the independent unions should be
direct or via SACTU.

The issues at stake were summarised in a resolution to the 1981
AGM which called for support for the independent unions in
addition to the traditional policy of supporting SACTU. It went on
to argue that the movement should "encourage the formation of
direct fraternal links between all independent non-racial trade
unions in South Africa and unions in Britain at all levels of union
organisation". It called on Anti-Apartheid to encourage exchange
visits with the independent unions.

The Anti-Apartheid executive successfully opposed this
proposal, confirming instead a previous policy document issued by
the movement. Existing policy was to "establish fraternal links
between South African and British workers through the South
African Congress of Trade Unions", something that should be
"continued and strengthened". Exchange visits were specifically
rejected, since the movement believed that because unions in South
Africa organise in what it termed "semi-legal or clandestine
conditions", direct links could "provoke harassment and in other
ways jeopardise these trade unionists' work".

SACTU entered the debate with an article in the April 1982 issue
of *Workers' Unity* entitled 'Direct Links Stink!' — claiming that
visits to South Africa by unions were objectionable since "they do
us no good and put our organisation in jeopardy". Similarly visits
from South African unions to the UK or USA were unnecessary
since the independent unions ". . . don't need lessons in class

collaboration". Most tellingly the article attacked direct links as an attempt to by-pass what it termed "the peoples' revolutionary organisations, the ANC(SA) and SACTU".

The argument was soon overtaken by events. Over the past eight years the independent unions had developed extensive links with the international labour movement. The Council of Unions of South Africa is now a full affiliate of the ICFTU. Many unions are affiliates of their appropriate International Trade Secretariat. The Metal and Allied Workers Union, for example, a member of FOSATU, is now an active participant in the work of the International Metalworkers Federation, successfully using this forum to secure the expulsion of certain racist South African unions from the ranks of the International.

In the UK these exchanges were given the blessing of the Labour Party in a guideline that was issued in 1982 (see Appendix 6). After consultation with a wide range of bodies, including the ICFTU, SACTU and ANC, CUSA and FOSATU, the Party endorsed exchanges between the union movements on condition that a distinction is drawn between the independent unions and unions such as TUCSA. Visits should only take place at the request of and according to a schedule drawn up in co-operation between British unions and the independent unions in South Africa.

A rather different aspect of the debate emerged from the South African unions themselves. After considerable discussion FOSATU sought to define its relations with other movements, and the liberation movements in particular. The speech by FOSATU General Secretary, Joe Foster, to the Federation's 1982 conference, crystallised the arguments (see Appendix 1).

While acknowledging the crucial role that the ANC played in organising the South African oppressed, irrespective of tribe, class or indeed race, Foster goes on to argue that there is a danger that the movement may, because of the broad class alliance that it represents, ultimately turn against the very workers that form the bulk of its support. Foster puts it in these terms: "All the great and successful popular movements have had as their aim the overthrow of oppressive — most often colonial — regimes. But these movements cannot and have not in themselves been able to deal with the particular and fundamental problems of workers. Their task is to remove regimes that are regarded as illegitimate and unacceptable by the majority. It is, therefore, essential that workers must strive to build their own powerful and effective organisation even whilst they are part of the wider popular struggle. This organisation is necessary to protect and further worker interests and to ensure that the popular movement is not hijacked by elements who will in the end have no option but to turn against their worker supporters".

A similar but less elaborate point was made by FOSATU President, Chris Dlamini. Following a visit to Zimbabwe he remarked that although some people in Zimbabwe were liberated, workers were not. This he put down to the absence of a strong workers' movement. "Worker liberation can only be achieved by a strong, well organised worker movement". Precisely what is meant by such a movement is a moot point. To what extent can unions fulfill what are essentially political roles? In a situation like South Africa, where the main political organisations of the oppressed are banned, what role can trade unions play? Clearly these are both complex and highly pertinent questions.

One answer to these questions was posed by a further article in *African Communist*. Deeply critical of the FOSATU position — which it labelled syndicalist — it reiterated the familiar arguments against regarding the working class as the sole force opposing the apartheid state. It went on to charge FOSATU with ignoring or even distorting history in failing to mention the role of the South African Communist Party. Far from there not being an organisation of the working class, the author charges that the unions are attempting to substitute themselves for the Communist Party which is ". . . a political party of the working class". The analysis goes on: "Dare FOSATU ignore this? And dare it ignore the confusion and division it will sow in the ranks of the working class if it sets up a new 'workers movement' in competition with or alongside the still living Communist Party?" (*African Communist*, No.83, second quarter 1983).

It is unclear whether these views represent official thinking on this subject. There appears to be some distance between such sentiments and recent statements of the ANC. An article in the ANC journal *Mayibuya* spelled out a clear call for unity amongst the trade unions — irrespective of their ideological concerns. There was a distinct absence of criticism of unions that sought to register with the state or have joined Industrial Councils. The statement called for 'flexibility' on the part of all concerned, in order to achieve a united movement. Differences of tactics on these issues ". . . must not be used as an issue to militate against unity".

In a recent interview, ANC president Oliver Tambo made it plain that his analysis was one in which the workers' movement was given equal importance with the armed confrontation with the state. While power "would not be achieved without armed struggle . . . it would be equally disastrous to say the armed struggle has no need of any other form of struggle. Organisation of the workers is most important", he declared.

This is a perspective that will have, if anything, been

strengthened by the new geopolitics of the region. The Nkomati accord between South Africa and Mozambique, the accommodation with Angola and the continued pressure on the other states bordering on South Africa must mean that the armed struggle will become increasingly difficult over the next few years. Although it is unlikely to invalidate this approach, it is likely to mean that the ANC will place increasing emphasis on other forms of struggle, including building the trade union movement. If, as now seems likely, a genuinely national trade union centre emerged, then the ANC will have no alternative but to come to some understanding with the union centre.

Political role of black unions

It would, however, be a mistake to see this as simply a debate conducted between FOSATU and the ANC. A number of other unions have joined the debate, and the subject has been broadened out to cover the whole question of the political role of the union movement. On one issue all the unions agree: that they have a political role. The question is how best to exercise this role. The FOSATU position, that the workers must first establish their own perspective and organisational capacity, was echoed by a number of other major unions, including the Food and Canning Workers and the General Workers Union. In particular both rejected calls to join the newly established political groupings which have emerged in South Africa. These groupings — the United Democratic Front (which follows a non-racial approach and is broadly sympathetic to the viewpoint of the ANC) and the National Forum Committee (which is in the black consciousness tradition, insisting on black leadership of the struggle against apartheid) — were formed to unite the opposition to apartheid. Both are amorphous bodies bringing together hundreds of small community and other organsations, from church groups and sports clubs to political parties and trade unions. It is the heterogeneous nature of the groupings that has been at least in part the cause of the mistrust that has arisen between them and some of the most important unions. In essence their calls for the unions to affiliate to them has met with three distinct responses.

The most established of the unions have rejected the call — those adopting this position include FOSATU, FCWU and GWU. From CUSA both groupings, the UDF and the NFC, have won acceptance. And the more community orientated unions such as SAAWU, Municipal and General Workers Union and the General and Allied Workers Union have joined only the UDF. But what do each of these stands mean?

The first position was elaborated by Dave Lewis, general secretarty of GWU in an extensive interview that he gave (see Appendix 2). He argued that the union was by no means saying that it rejected politics, and even that it encouraged its members to become involved in organisations that were affiliated to bodies such as the UDF. But he ruled out affiliation by the union for two distinct reasons. Firstly he pointed out that as a union leader he had to represent his members in a very strong sense. He had to ensure that he always acted on a mandate from them. And this was simply not the case for most of the organisations that were affiliates of the UDF. This made co-operation with them difficult, since it was not possible to always get a mandate from his membership before being involved in a particular decision taken by such bodies such as the UDF. This was made more difficult because within the GWU were members who supported different political positions, and Lewis was not prepared to alienate one section of the union by affiliating to a body of which they did not approve. The second objection was because of the multi-class nature of the UDF. He argued that because of this it was very difficult for workers to become involved. Workers were simply not used to the kind of structures, or sufficiently educated to fully participate in the life of political bodies such as the UDF. For example, most of the discussions were in English, a language that many workers did not understand. For this reason their participation would of necessity be limited.

"Given the above, there is a feeling on the part of the workers that they will not be able to participate fully in the decisions that lead to a programme of action, and this is an anathema to an organised worker. They are not going to be drawn into an organisation in which they feel that they will have to take action blindly, without having participated in the decision making. Those are really the key aspects of the class composition of the organisations: firstly, that we draw our membership from a very wide and diverse range of political views, unlike most of the other organisations participating in the UDF, and secondly, that our members are working class people, and as working class they come from a culture that is very distinct from that of other more privileged classes in society".

At the same time Lewis stressed that the union was prepared to participate in campaigns with the UDF, and said that he did not rule out the possibility of a national trade union centre affiliating to such a body.

The position of CUSA was rather different (see Appendix 5). It too was approached by the UDF and the NFC early in 1983, with requests for affiliation. After discussion of the issues involved by their executive committee the following resolution was adopted on 30 April 1983:

"Having examined the proposals of the regime on the constitution;

Having further examined the basis of the call by various organisations regarding the constitutional proposals;

Noting that the Nationalist Party is presently in disarray and that these proposals may therefore be changed to impose White rule under different guise even through a referendum;

Knowing that the White opposition forces and parties are themselves divided and without any effect;

The Council of Unions of South Arica now therefore:

● wishes to place on record its complete and total rejection of the proposal;
● pledges itself to participate in every forum to work towards the achievement of a just and democratic society;
● calls upon its members to lend their individual support to all efforts of community organisations to end this foolish plan;
● pledges itself to all forces and all efforts to work towards a common citizenship in an undivided democratic and just society."

CUSA went on to state that: "Following the response of various unions and the nature of press reports together with intransigent positions adopted by some sections of the community CUSA is involved currently on an ongoing examination of its attitude and role in the UDC and NFC". Quite what this intransigence was, or the nature of the examination conducted by CUSA, is not stated. But the general thrust of their position is clear. They would support any organisation that opposed the new constitutional proposals, and would work with them for the achievement of a just and democratic society.

The third position, of affiliation to the UDF only, was defended by the Municipal and General Workers Union of South Africa, amongst others (see Appendix 3). They pointed out that a trade union is not a political party, and as such is limited in the range of questions that it is capable of tackling. They also said that no political party could be exclusively composed of working class members, and that even if it were there was no guarantee that it would act in the interests of workers. In addition there was the problem of the rural areas, areas in which the unions could not function, and for this reason a body like the UDF was vital if a broadly based opposition to apartheid was to be created.

A similar argument was put foward by the General and Allied Workers Union, whose general secretary, Sydney Mufamadi, stated: "Some want to perceive the working class as only found on the factory floor. Our view is that even those people who are not behind machines on the factory floor can be said to be waging a working class struggle if the issues which they take up in their various sites of struggle, and the way in which they take those issues up, serve to undermine the class relations upon which the present society is built . . . Ideologically speaking, we are saying that we are involved in a national democratic struggle wherein we put special emphasis on the leadership role which has to be played by the working class. If you look at the UDF declaration, there is nothing there which negates the interests of the working class. We feel that we as a trade union have got room in the UDF as much as any other organisation, be it operating in the community, at a student level or in the women's front.''

Just as the FOSATU position leaves questions unanswered, so do the positions outlined above. For they fail to take up the points made by the GWU. In particular they do not deal with the problems faced by workers participating in multi-class organisations, even if they are formally open to workers. Nor does it meet the point about the kind of mandate that union leaders have from their members.

It would appear, therefore, that all of the unions still have major problems to overcome before the trade unions can fulfil their true potential within the South African political economy. It is unlikely that these difficulties will be resolved in theory. Rather, it will be in facing the real issues of the day that the unions, and the political movements that seek their support, will unpack these problems. It may be that once a national union centre comes into being that the unions will have the confidence that they need to move from their current positions. Perhaps in the end it will take an event, such as the tragic death of Niel Aggett, to bring the movement together on a political front. But when they do, then the enormous strength that is now being forged will, for the first time, be seen in action.

Chapter 11

International Solidarity

The importance of international solidarity with black workers in South Africa can never be underestimated; nor should it be overplayed. South Africa's white-dominated economy and political culture seeks integration with and acceptance by Western capitalism. The regime does respond to international pressure. Particularly effective have been the sporting boycotts and the expulsion of South Africa from most world bodies. Another factor that has had to be constantly taken into account by the authorities and big business is the haphazard disinvestment campaign in some countries, notably in Scandanavia and in a few American companies where shareholders with what could be described as a conscience have been subject to moral and church originated pressure. The collapse of the Portuguese colonies of Mozambique and Angola by 1975, and the disappearance of the white settler regime in Zimbabwe by 1980 added to a sense of international isolation. No-one disputed (or disputes) the overwhelming economic and military domination that South Africa enjoys in the southern half of the continent but the solidarity of most African countries in denying South Africa economic, or even transport, links (except obviously in the cases of the front line states where these were of a lifeblood necessity) also added pressure on the South African state.

The clear identification of the Carter administration in the United States between 1976 and 1980 and especially Carter's UN ambassador, Andrew Young, with the politics of human rights and, to a more hesitant extent, those of black liberation left South Africa uncertain about the attitude of the most important capitalist power, in the key years during which Pretoria was elaborating its response to the challenge posed by the growth of an organised black working class after 1973. The important role of foreign capital in South Africa also opened the way to solidarity pressure of all sorts in the countries where the headquarters of banks and multinationals with subsidiaries in South Africa were based.

It was against this background that the emerging black trade union movement worked out its strategy of international links and solidarity in the 1970s and 1980s. By the middle of the 1980s they had had a decade of experience of international contacts and were able to judge those that would be of direct use. At the same time unions in Europe and North America and their international organisations were able to go beyond angry denunciations of apartheid in national and world forums and instead looked to concrete ways of helping the black workers in South Africa.

Solidarity during disputes

Car workers at the Volkswagen plant in Uitenhage, for example, had established good links with the 2.5 million-strong West German metalworkers' union, IG Metall. These proved of value in June 1980, when black workers launched a three-week strike at the VW plants. Organised by unions affiliated to FOSATU, the strike centred on wage demands and shop steward rights. At its height the dispute involved 7,500 workers in 11 factories and a mass march was broken by riot police firing shotguns and teargas.

In Germany, IG Metall applied pressure on the parent company. In this, they were helped by the German industrial democracy system which placed the president of the union on the supervisory board of Volkswagen; he thus had direct access to the highest level of VW management. The union also informed VW workers about what the company was doing. The International Metalworkers Federation, to which the South African and German unions are affiliated raised funds for the strike and £38,000 was transferred to South Africa. An assistant general secretary of the federation flew from its headquarters in Geneva to provide what help he could. In fact, as one of the international labour movement's most experienced economists he was able to advise the unions during the negotiations and in preparing their claim for a living wage index to replace the previously applied minimum standard of living index.

As an outcome of the strike the workers gained a wage increase of up to 40 per cent and Volkswagen and the other automobile companies in the Eastern Cape agreed to continue talks on the union's proposals for a new living wage index. The number of wage categories was reduced and Ford and General Motors agreed to the same scales. For the American multinationals there was the knowledge that the workers in Port Elizabeth had established close contacts with the United Auto Workers union in Detroit. Marc Stepp, the black UAW Vice-President, visited the South African auto union in December 1981.

Another important result concerned trade union rights at plant level which led to the recognition of paid shop stewards and in-plant training for an increased number of African workers. Subsequently three full-time shop stewards were elected, becoming full-time worker representatives while still being on the company payroll. The elections were the first of their kind in South Africa. The Volkswagen shop stewards have now established a telex link with their opposite numbers in Wolfsburg, the West German centre of VW production.

Britain, Sweden, Italy

In 1981, support was gained by workers in British Leyland's South African subsidiary. An attempt to dismiss 2,000 workers at Leyland's plants in Cape Town resulted in the intervention by British trade union officials. At a meeting with the parent company in Britain, Alex Kitson, Deputy General Secretary of the Transport & General Workers' Union and Terry Duffy, President of the Amalgamated Union of Engineering Workers protested to the management about the behaviour of the South African subsidiary. The intervention was successful and subsequently many of the dismissed workers were re-employed. In 1982, action in support of the South African Allied Workers' Union claim for recognition with the South African Rowntree's Mackintosh subsidiary occurred at all levels of the British labour movement, with statements by TUC General Secretary, Len Murray, and local action with shop-stewards at Rowntree's headquarters in York.

The International Union of Foodworkers (IUF) mobilised its 183 affiliated unions around a threatened boycott of Coca Cola after a Port Elizabeth firm holding the local Coca Cola franchise dismissed workers belonging to the General Workers Union after they had gone on strike for higher wages and union recognition. The IUF pressure worked with the firm taking back some of the fired workers and permitting union activities in the plant.

In 1975, the Swedish national trade union centre, LO, published a lengthy report on Swedish companies' involvement in South Africa. The influential Swedish trade union movement has quietly, but effectively, put pressure on firms such as SKF and Electrolux to recognise and deal fairly with the emerging unions operating in their South African subsidiaries.

In 1983, the powerful Italian metalworkers' union, the 800,000-strong Federazione Lavoratori Metalmeccanici (FLM) played a decisive role in successfully helping black car workers when their union, the National Automobile and Allied Workers Union (NAAWU) was in dispute with the South African subsidiary of Alfa Romeo. The South African management had refused to recognise the union. Unlike the Port Elizabeth factories, the automobile multinationals with plants in Transvaal were strongly resisting union recognition. NAAWU contacted the FLM in Italy and a NAAWU official flew to Rome for the meeting between the

Alfa Romeo management, the FLM and, the International Metal-workers Federation, to which both unions belong. As a result of this meeting, the union was recognised at two of the Alfa Romeo plants in South Africa and was given facilities and access to the third for organising purposes. The 1984 report by the ILO's Director General hailed this as "a unique agreement . . . the first to be achieved outside the country. It occurred in Rome and illustrated the effectiveness of international support. The significance of this development lies in the speed and unanimity with which the trade union groups involved were able to act in support of the South African union".

Clearly in each of the above cases it was the determination of the black workers themselves that achieved positive results. But the action of trade unionists outside South Africa is a legitimate, useful contribution in defence of the demands of South Africa's independent unions.

The value of solidarity action has long been understood by the trade union movement, both nationally and internationally. At all levels of the labour movement strategies for assistance and support of the rights of trade unionists throughout the world have been discussed and policies outlined. South Africa is no exception and rarely does a conference of trade union members occur in which condemnation of the apartheid system is not high on the agenda of international issues.

Bodies such as the International Labour Office (ILO) and the International Confederation of Free Trade Unions (ICFTU) have formulated comprehensive programmes to encourage international action in support of black workers' rights. At a conference in November 1980 held in the TUC's headquarters in London, the ICFTU proposed a plan of "internationally co-ordinated action . . . to prevent the South African union movement from strangulation". The programme offers assistance to black trade unions in the forms of "financial, technical, legal and relief aid, as well as political support". The ICFTU urged the international trade secretariats, individual unions and shop floor workers to support the struggle of black workers to gain recognition agreements for their unions, and during labour disputes in South Africa "by appropriate solidarity action e.g. intervention with headquarters management, boycotts, etc."

In January 1984, the ICFTU held a second conference (at the Dusseldorf head office of the German Trade Union Confederation (DGB)), to evaluate and update the programme of action in support of the emerging independent and non-racial unions. The conference was attended by union leaders around the world and included representatives from the South African unions (both

CUSA and FOSATU). Warning that as the independent movement grows, so South Africa's repression of the unions will intensify, the conference reiterated the urgent need to offer financial, legal and technical aid, combined with increased solidarity in defence of the rights of South Africa's workers.

International Labour Organisation

As the major international agency dealing with labour matters the ILO is another important forum in which the rights of the independent union movement can be defended. A tripartite United Nations body bringing together representatives from government, employers and labour organisations, the ILO adopted a Declaration on Apartheid in 1964. Periodically updated the Declaration calls for action to increase ILO educational and technical assistance to black workers and their independent unions. The ILO regularly condemns the apartheid regime and intervenes in specific cases protesting at violation of basic human and trade union rights. In addition the ILO publishes an annual 'Special Report' on South Africa which is a valuable source of information about labour relations in the Republic covering a wide range of issues; union structure, industrial relations legislation, strikes and repressive measures. The ILO has also served indirectly to bring home to South African employers the anger in the world community over the effect of apartheid on labour practices. In the late 1970s, the South African Association of Chambers of Commerce (ASSOCOM) were able to attend the ILO's tripartitie Committee on Apartheid as observers with the employer's group. They had to listen to ferocious attacks from both workers and government representatives. As a result of this meeting the Association sent out a circular in 1980 urging the National Manpower Commission to "examine ways and means whereby registration of Trade Unions can be made more attractive and whereby the existing stigma and suggestion that government wishes to 'control' the unions can be removed". The Association also said that freedom of association was an absolute right and that a union's racial composition should be entirely a matter for the union and not the government. The submission went on to state there should be "no right of veto with regard to the membership of the Industrial Councils. This is a subject which has caused considerable criticism both within and without the Republic and it is difficult to defend." As Dr Christopher Hill, director of the Centre of Southern African Studies at the University of York noted: "All these points had been made forcefully at the ILO meeting. The fact that ASSOCOM's Secretary chose to repeat them in a circular to members suggests that his attendance at Geneva had not been fruitless".

Material assistance and help with education

Material assistance is equally important to the independent trade unions. Financial assistance is made all the more important by the South African government's attempts to curb the flow of external funds to the independent unions. The ICFTU and the International Trade Secretariats have managed to give some cash to the emerging unions. CUSA, as an ICFTU affiliate has received direct help. FOSATU has not formally affiliated to any international federation but its affiliates are members of International Trade Secretariats and receive financial support — often in the form of travel and organisation costs — indirectly through them. Money from overseas is a sensitive subject as with it comes the suggestion of control and ideological alignment. In one instance the offer of a handsome sum of money from one source was refused by all the emerging unions because, as one spokesman put it: "It was crude and obvious that the national centre concerned would want to proclaim to the world that the black unions were 'their boys'." In fact, cash assistance has come from left-wing unions in Scandinavia, Italy and France, as well as those whose political outlook is not conceptually hostile to capitalism as in the United States.

Material assistance can mean more than mere cash. The highly developed trade union education programmes available in the industrialised countries can offer the independent unions of South Africa a valuable resource. Officials from the emerging unions have been sent on courses at Ruskin College, Oxford and union education schools in West Europe and the United States where they can learn the basics of bargaining skills and trade union organisation. Unions have also been able to send education specialists to South Africa to help with shop steward courses, especially in the area of health and safety.

Codes of conduct

The use of codes of conduct has been urged as an effective means to defend trade union rights in South Africa. The operation of the codes, established by the European Economic Community and the United States (the so-called Sullivan code named after the Rev. Leon Sullivan who proposed it) have proved to be a disappointment. None of the independent or non-racial unions have expressed any confidence in either of the Codes or believe that they have helped unions establish their presence or improve wages or conditions. The main fault with the Codes is that it is difficult to monitor them and their application is voluntary and moral, rather than obligatory and legal.

In 1983, the British government reported that it has received replies from 130 British companies under the EEC Code of Conduct. No company by company details were provided, only a generalised summary. However the *Observer* newspaper obtained details of certain company reports which showed that in 1981 important British metal companies such as British Electric Traction, Guest Keen and Nettlefold, Turner and Newall were paying workers below what was considered to be the minimum poverty line.

The 1982 Sullivan Code report noted that 142 United States companies operating in South Africa were not even signatories to the Code and of 93 signatory companies 29 did not bother to report. Although the reporting companies said they had de-segregated workplace facilities and many said they supported the right of their workers to join a union, others indicated that they did not approve of trade unions in general, considering them to be unnecessary.

It is widely agreed within the trade union movement and indeed by their chief advocates like the Rev. Sullivan that without legal enforcement the codes will remain largely ineffectual. At the Dusseldorf conference the ICFTU confirmed that the results of the Codes remained totally inadequate and urged that legal enforcement be implemented to ensure "that companies that breach the codes are penalised".

At its most basic level solidarity action is the abhorence of the cruel tactics employed by the South African state in defence of white suprematism. Every year communications appealing to the United Nations, or protesting to the Republic's Prime Minister, P.W. Botha, are sent from the trade union movement, internationally, nationally and locally. With tragic regularity pickets are held outside the South African embassy in Trafalgar Square, London. In 1982 further need for such solidarity occurred; the death of Neil Aggett and the detention of SAAWU's leadership are examples of a wave of repression in the 1980s. Protests by telegram may seem futile but to a detainee they are a source of invaluable encouragement and continue to embarrass the Pretoria regime. A useful example of solidarity support has been the long-running campaign by the British technicians and draughtsmen's union, AUEU-TASS for the release of their member, Dave Kitson. Kitson, who had dual British-South African nationality was sentenced to 20 years' imprisonment in 1964 because of his involvement with SACTU and the ANC. He was released shortly before the full term expired in May 1984. He said that by the end of his term he was receiving so many solidarity Christmas cards sent by trade unionists from overseas that the prison governor complained about the effect it was having on the prison postal service!

Contact established through international solidarity can also provide unexpected benefits to the independent unions in South Africa. At an international conference in Washington in May 1981 delegates from black metal unions in South Africa held a meeting with shop floor representatives of the Polish Solidarity union. After Solidarity was suppressed following General Jaruzelski's coup in December 1981, many Polish workers fled as refugees to Austria. There, recruiters from South African firms sought immigrants with specific, needed skills. The black unions in South Africa contacted the underground leadership of Solidarity and together with Lech Walesa they appealed to Polish workers in West Europe not to emigrate to South Africa and stressing the common struggle of workers in South Africa and Poland for human and trade union rights.

Union visits

The question of visits to and from South Africa by trade unionists has often excited controversy. Ill-informed trade union officials from Europe or North America who spent more time with old-style white union leaders or with employer and government representatives rather than with black workers caused harm and confusion. Visits by certain blacks with trade union posts who seemed to support some of the government's policies also created problems for unions overseas who were uncertain as to the exact shape of the policies and solidarity needs of the emerging trade unions. As noted in Chapter 10, the problem was further complicated by statements from organisations falsely claiming that only government stooges were allowed out of South Africa or trying to assert that they should be the sole conduit of help to the black workers.

As usual the best judge of the usefulness of visits are the independent unions themselves. In the automobile industry the major black unions issued this formal statement in 1981: "We strongly favour fraternal contact between workers in South Africa and workers in other countries, at all levels, provided this is guided by the interests and requirements of workers. The aims of these visits should be to strengthen fraternal ties between organised workers in different countries and to carry forward the struggle in South Africa to win the same rights as have been won by workers in other countries".

Partly in response to the debate about the viability of direct contact and visits to South Africa in 1982 the British Labour Party's National Executive issued a set of guidelines (in the form of an 'advice note' to affiliated organisations). The guidelines endorsed direct contacts and visits provided that they occurred as a result of requests from *bona fide* independent or non-racial unions. The statement followed a detailed examination of the issues by the Labour Party's Africa Committee which received submissions from many trade union sources including key South African unions such as CUSA and FOSATU (see Appendix 6).

The largest of the International Trade Secretariats, the International Metalworkers Federation urged, in 1984, its 170 affiliates: "to extend solidarity with South African workers by encouraging the development of appropriate company-to-company workplace links and organising visits to and from South Africa by plant-level union leaders. Visits to South Africa should be carefully prepared in full consultation with the unions in South Africa". In the meantime, black workers were taking advantage of their international links to go overseas. FOSATU's president, Chris Dlamini, for example, was a guest of the French socialist union confederation CFDT at their congress in 1982. James Motlatsi, president of the National Union of Mineworkers, made useful contacts at the congress of the Miners International Federation, held in Luxembourg in May 1984. British unions, including the Transport and General Workers Union, the Association of Scientific, Technical and Managerial Staffs and the General Municipal and Boilermakers Union as well as the TUC hosted a visit by Maxwell Zulu, Moses Mayekiso and Geoff Schreiner, Transvaal and Natal branch officers of the Metal and Allied Workers Union in March 1984. As well as taking part in union education courses, they established contact with shop stewards from many companies that their union was organising in South Africa, including Metal Box, Dunlop, Lucas, GEC and Chloride. Black trade unionists have made similar visits to West Germany, Sweden, Denmark, the Netherlands, the United States and Canada.

At the best of time effective solidarity is not easy to achieve and it is not only the South African government that wishes to obstruct the links being established between the independent unions and the international trade union movement. In many Western countries trade union solidarity for workers abroad is shackled by legislation designed to destroy the power of organised labour. In Britain, the 1982 Employment Act prevents British workers taking action in sympathy with trade unionists engaged in disputes overseas. The Act makes it unlawful for workers in Britain to take action unless the British workers are 'likely to be affected' by the outcome of the dispute abroad. Thus a union in Britain wanting to take action in support of black workers in South Africa working for the same multinational company will be blocked. The courts would have to decide whether the outcome of the South African dispute would be likely to affect the British workers' terms and conditions of employment. If the case is lost there can be no legal trade dispute and no immunity if the company takes court action against the union involved.

In protest at the Employment Act, TUC General Secretary, Len Murray wrote to the Prime Minister, Mrs Margaret Thatcher and urged the Government to withdraw its legislation. Stressing the international dimension he complained that it will be illegal for trade unionists "to take action in support of fellow trade unionists in other countries — such as Poland or South Africa — in their struggle for freedom and dignity''.

Despite such obstacles solidarity has succeeded in advancing the workers' struggle in South Africa. The instances of solidarity action described above during the disputes at Volkswagen, Coca Cola, Alfa Romeo and Rowntree are amongst just a few examples and have been chosen largely because they represent a degree of success. Doubtless it is easy to list the failures, the disappointments and the unfulfilled expectations. However, the call for assistance in defence of trade union rights and the urgency for response is ever present. As the trade union movement worldwide struggles to maintain its strength, the need to gain confidence from success is paramount.

In South Africa, the independent unions are growing and challenging apartheid's denial of their democratic rights. Opponents of that 'crime against humanity' must offer their commitment and support to the independent unions. The battle they are engaged in, as Joe Foster, General Secretary of FOSATU, comments "is part of the wider struggle". In South Africa, as elsewhere, an independent and democratic trade union movement and a repressive state are fundamentally incompatible.

Chapter 12

Conclusion

May day 1984 saw the first mass celebrations of the international workers' day in South Africa for nearly 30 years. In Cape Town, 3,000 workers were packed into a crowded hall for a meeting organised by different unions. In Natal, thousands wore May Day stickers and distributed leaflets to workers explaining the historic importance of May Day. As usual, very little of this activity was reported by the South African media and no foreign correspondent deemed such workers' celebrations worth a line.

By contrast, the coverage of the visit made by the South African premier, P.W. Botha, to some West European capitals a month later suggested that an event of almost world importance has taken place. Yet Botha, despite having shaken hands with Mrs Thatcher, Herr Kohl and the Pope, flew back to a South Africa where a black working class was growing stronger in terms of its organisation, its self-development and the confidence that comes from successful struggle, as well as the experience that comes from problems and setbacks.

As we have tried to show, the range and depth of activities of the independent trade unions in South Africa is remarkable. The black working class has forced the South African state and capital to grant concessions which mark a significant, enduring increase in black power in the country. Each effort to co-opt the emerging trade union movement has been swept aside. Black workers have displayed an impressive maturity in judging how to handle state initiatives or how and when to use state industrial relations machinery. Commentators predicted that the recession and consequent unemployment of the 1980s would weaken union strength and reduce worker militancy. The reverse appears to have happened with strikes over pay, as well as job security, being as high in the first months of 1984 as they were in the preceding three years. The potential for growth is enormous. In the manufacturing, mining, and distribution sectors four of five workers are still not union members. When and if a united federation of unions is set up and is seen to be functioning on a continuing basis, its strength will speed up union organisation. Many black workers currently in TUCSA unions, and held there because of closed shop provisions, are likely to transfer to an independent federation.

If the independent unions have been successful in organisation and negotiation they have not been able to prevent the government continuing to implement, and in many cases, worsen the effects of the apartheid system. If you talk to most black workers and ask what is the outstanding event of the recent past they invariably answer: 'Soweto'. The 1976 revolt left 700 dead and a generation of young blacks permanently alienated. That anger is there, deep, rarely visible but it constitutes a hatred of apartheid and a burning desire to see it done away with, violently if need be; that hatred is a factor that transcends the objects of traditional trade unionism. It is a factor of which the white rulers of South Africa are perfectly well aware. Today's impressive level of black trade union organisation in South Africa has a precarious fragility and given the country's history it would be foolish to dismiss the possibility of outright suppression. In this context the need for labour movement organisations in the democratic countries to develop their links and solidarity with the black trade unions in South Africa becomes ever more urgent.

Yet violent suppression is not inevitably written into the future scripts. The Afrikaans mentality has been that of the laager, the self-protective ring against external pressure. In the early 19th century Afrikaners and blacks fought, sometimes side by side, against the encroachment of imperial Britain. The Boer War is hailed as an example of sturdy independence against a foreign master. The Nationalist victory of 1948 was the triumph of Afrikanerdom — of the white tribe of Southern Africa — over the power of the English speakers, whose loyalty was divided between England and South Africa. Since 1960, South Africa has devised an image for internal consumption which sees itself defending Western values against a communist wave from the northern liberated black African states. South African newspapers still use the word 'red' or 'reds' in headlines when referring to the Soviet Union. Now all this appears meaningless. The border states seem powerless, indeed are obliged to sign humiliating agreements with South Africa. The only threat to Afrikanerdom comes from within. Internal pressure is harder to deal with than a commonly perceived external menace. If change is to come to South Africa it will do so as a result of what happens inside the country. In that process, the organised black working class is likely to play a decisive role.

Appendix 1

The Workers' Struggle — Where Does FOSATU Stand?

The following document is the full text of the keynote address, given by the FOSATU General Secretary, Joe Foster, at the FOSATU Congress in April 1982, and endorsed by Congress as FOSATU policy.

Introduction

Three years ago — almost to the day — we met in this very same place to form FOSATU. Today we have set as our theme — the Workers' Struggle — in a serious attempt to further clarify where we as worker representatives see FOSATU to stand in this great struggle.

That we are discussing this theme today and resolutions that relate to it is a justification of our original decision to form FOSATU and shows how seriously we take the new challenges that face us three years after that decision. Clearly any such discussion raises many very important issues and the purpose of this paper is to try and bring together these issues in ways that will help guide our discussions.

It is the task of this Congress to give a clear policy direction to our actions between now and the next Congress — we believe that the issues raised in this paper are crucial to a political understanding of our policies and what we hope to achieve by them. We also believe that it is the task of Congress to add and modify the views expressed through open and serious debate.

FOSATU — an Assessment

In the three years that FOSATU has existed there is little doubt that we have achieved a lot in terms of growth and gains made for our members. However, I believe that our greatest achievement is the fact that at this Congress we are determined to re-evaluate our policies. We are determined to respond to new challenges and set new directions if this is necessary. We could have made this Congress a great occasion open to all to parade our successes and hide our failures, however, we have chosen otherwise.

We have chosen to keep it closed and to once again self-critically examine our position. I believe that this shows our determination to take the great militancy of our members and use this to build a just and fair society controlled by workers.

We have no intention of becoming self-satisfied trade unionists incapable of giving political direction to the workers struggle.

Yet we would only be dreaming of change if we do not strengthen and build our unions into large and effective organisations.

At our Inaugural Congress we stressed certain policies and set ourselves the task of establishing a tight federation of non-racial, national, industrial unions, based on shop floor strength. We set ourselves the task of sharing resources between affiliates and of building up an educational programme. We further stressed our independence in regard to party political organisations and from international trade union organisations.

Now it is not my task to assess every success and failure of FOSATU. There are reports tabled that will allow delegates to draw their own conclusions. However, it is important to make certain assessments in order to go further and identify why we need to clarify our position and set new clearer directions.

I believe that we have to ask ourselves two crucial questions:
— have we established an effective organisation based on shop floor strength and national non-racial industrial unions?
— has our organisational activity developed worker leadership that can give guidance and direction to all workers?

In answer to both questions it would be wrong to expect a positive answer after only three years. However, we should be able to assess if we are going in the right direction.

Clearly in regard to the first question we made progress — it could even be said to be considerable progress — with NAAWU, NUTW and MAWU beginning to be a significant presence in what are major industries. However, there is a long way to go both in these cases and more so in those of the other affiliates.

It is, however, the second question that poses more problems. As the unions grow and are faced with new challenges it becomes crucial that the leadership knows what direction it is going in. What are the organisational strategies that are necessary as the unions become larger and more effective. What dangers to worker militancy lie in recognition and stability?

As these unions grow then the question is what role do they play in the wider political arena. There has been a great upsurge in political activities over the last few years and many different political groups are looking to the union movement to state its position. We must be sure our organisation and our leadership can confidently state *its* position and continue to organise in the way that will strengthen and not weaken that position.

The purpose of this paper is to set out the issues we should debate if we are to meet the challenges.

Working Class Movement

As a trade union federation we are clearly concerned with workers and their aspirations. If we were to think in terms of our members only, we would have a very limited political role. If, however, we are thinking more widely of the working class then we have to examine very much more carefully what our political role is. In particular we need to look at this role in the South African context.

If we look at the advanced industrial countries then we see what can be called working class movements. There are a number of different organisations — trade unions, co-operatives, political parties and newspapers — that all see themselves as linked to the working class and furthering its interests. These working class movements are, therefore, powerful social forces in those societies.

In the capitalist economies these working class movements have power and organisation yet politically the working class is still subject to policies and practices that are clearly against their interests as the activities of Thatcher and Reagan show. This is increasingly leading to intense political and organisational activity to give the working class and the union movement a clearer direction so as to gather together the working class movement into a force that will more definitely put workers in control of their own destiny.

In the Socialist countries similar battles are being fought. Whilst social, political and economic relations in these countries have been greatly altered and there have been great achievements to the benefit of workers, there is still the need for workers themselves to control their own destiny. So Solidarity was not struggling to restore capitalism in Poland, its struggle was to establish more democratic worker control over *their* socialist society.

Now my purpose in briefly looking at the working class movement in the advanced industrial countries was twofold:

Firstly, so that we can be clear that worker activities such as strikes and protests do not in themselves mean that a working class movement or working class politics exist. These latter are more than that — they are large-scale organisations with a clear social and political identity as the working class.

Secondly, I wished to show that the pure size of working class organisation is itself no guarantee that workers will control their own destiny. In fact as the struggle of Solidarity shows, even the fact that a country is said to be socialist does not guarantee that workers control their own destiny.

In short it could be said that workers must build a powerful and effective movement if they are to succeed in advancing their interests against some very hostile forces, but they must also ensure that this movement is able to take a clear political direction.

The experience of the great working class movements in the advanced industrial countries is a very important guide and lesson to us. However, it cannot provide all our answers. Firstly, in South Africa we cannot talk of a working class movement as we have defined it above. Secondly, whilst there is undoubtedly a large and growing working class its power is only a potential power since as yet it has no definite social identity of itself as working class.

The questions we should, therefore, address ourselves to, are:
— Why has no working class movement emerged?
— What are the prospects for such a movement emerging?
— What role can FOSATU play in such a process?

Political History and Workers

It is not possible in a paper such as this to deal fully with all the developments in South Africa's history that have led to the non-existence of workers' movement in South Africa.

South Africa's history has been characterised by great repression and the major political and ideological *instrument* for this repression has been *racism*. Yet the major effect of this repression has been to very rapidly establish a large capitalist economy.

Racism and the violence and injustices associated with it is a very stark and clear form of repression. Alongside this only about 5-10 per cent of the population has ever had the franchise. Clearly, therefore, there is a very identifiable oppressive force and the major political task of the oppressed people has always been to attack that oppressive and racist regime.

So what has developed in South Africa is a very powerful tradition of popular or populist politics. The role of the great political movements such as the ANC and the Congress Alliance has been to mobilise the masses against the repressive minority regime. In such a situation mass mobilisation is essential so as to challenge the legitimacy of the state both internally and internationally.

Where virtually all the population is voteless and oppressed by a racial minority then a great alliance of all classes is both necessary and a clear political strategy. Furthermore, building such an alliance was a great task.

The ANC had to overcome racial division so as to rise above the divisive racism of the oppressors. They had to deal with opportunistic tribal leadership, to organise thousands upon thousands of people and they had to do all this in the face of harsh repression by the state. In achieving this there is little wonder that the ANC rose to be one of the great liberation movements in Africa.

In this context it is also easier to see and understand why the trade-union movement acted in a particular way. The racial divisions in the working class, linked as they were to other objective factors, made it possible for capital to quite quickly suppress any serious challenge to their supremacy. It was possible to create the conditions that led to a politically tame union movement and thereby forced more militant and progressive unions to bear the brunt of state action, which in turn affected the politics of these unions.

Furthermore, at all times there were occasions when workers resisted by strike action, protest and organisation. Yet this by itself cannot constitute a working class movement. Whilst the unions were often prominent they were always small and weakly organised both nationally and in the factories. They could not provide an organisational base for a working class movement as we have defined it above.

Progressive and militant unions were continually the subject of state harassment, but, never managed to seriously challenge capital nationally or on a sustained basis. As a result the effective political role of progressive unions and of worker activity was to provide a crucial part of any popular struggle and that was to give it its 'Worker Voice'. No mass popular movement can be effective or be seen to be effective if it does not have some worker involvement or representation. By the 1950s with the growth of South Africa's industry and the size of the working class the need to include workers became essential and as a result SACTU became an important element of the Congress Alliance.

In these circumstances the progressive trade unions became part of the popular struggle against oppression. They did not and probably could not have provided the base for working class organisation. There is of course no doubt that their activities have been very, very important in creating the conditions that led to the emergence in the last 10 to 15 years of the present progressive trade unions. However, these unions are operating in a different environment.

Workers and their struggle became very much part of the wider popular struggle. An important effect of this development was that capital could hide behind the curtains of apartheid and racism. The political energies of the oppressed masses and of international critics were focused on the apartheid regime and its abhorrent racism. The government and Afrikanerdom became the focus of attack. In fact the position was such that learned liberal academics saw in capital the great hope for change despite the fact that capital and its lackeys were undoubtedly the major beneficiaries of apartheid.

Capital did its very best to keep in the political background and as a result this helped prevent the creation of capital's logical political opposite which is a working class political movement. However, of crucial significance was that capital was growing rapidly and changing its very nature into a more monopolistic, technologically advanced and concentrated form. Its links internationally were also growing as was its importance for international capital.

We find, therefore, that behind the scenes of the great battle between apartheid regime and its popular opponents that the capitalist economy has flourished and capital emerges now as a powerful and different force. It
— is highly concentrated in truly gigantic corporations;
— has access to international information on how to deal with working class challenges;
— has access to the state's security information;
— is able to rapidly share and assess information;
— is able to use the objective circumstances in its favour such as unemployment and influx control to weaken worker organisations;
— is now an important part of international capital and cannot therefore, be lightly discarded by international capital;
— is able to hide behind politics and as a result can hide its sophisticated attacks on labour because no-one is paying any attention.

Yet as the upsurge of popular political activity emerged again in the 1970s some of its new forms such as Black Consciousness also place little emphasis on capital. So there is a growing gap between popular politics and the power of capital and as a result the potential power of workers. It is in this context we should look at the likelihood of a working class politics emerging.

Need for a Working Class Movement

The growing size of the economy and the dramatic changes taking place in capital have created important new conditions in the economy. We also have to take into account the speed and manner in which the economy has developed. In discussing the working class movements in the advanced industrial economies, we have to bear in mind that in most cases they took about 100 years or more to fully develop. Industry started first by building larger and larger factories and bringing people together in these factories.

The new capitalists had to struggle politically with the older ruling classes over labour, land, taxation policy, tariff protection, political rights and political power.

The mechanisation became more important and there was a definite change in production processes. As this happened the skilled workers who had usually given leadership to the craft unions found themselves in a very difficult position. As a result leadership problems in the organisation of trade unions and the political environment, developed in a complex and relatively slow way.

In South Africa this has been condensed into 60-70 years and from the outset large scale capitalist enterprises dominated. The birth of capitalism here was brutal and quick. The industrial proletariat was ripped from its land in the space of a few decades. At present capitalist production massively dominates all other production. There are no great landlords on their agricultural estates and there is no significant peasantry or collective agriculture. Virtually everyone depends for all or part of their income on industry or capitalist agriculture.

The working class have experienced a birth of fire in South Africa and they constitute the major objective political force opposed to the state and capital. There is no significant petty bourgeoisie or landed class with an economic base in our society.

In the economy capital and labour are the major forces, yet politically the struggle is being fought elsewhere.

The existence of this industrial proletariat and the rapid transformation of capital are very powerful reasons why a working class movement could rapidly develop in South Africa. There are a number of factors that will assist in the organisation of workers:

— the great concentration of capital has also meant a greater concentration of workers. These workers generally have a higher level of basic education and skills than before and their links with the past are all but broken so that more and more a worker identity is emerging:

— this is reinforced by the sophisticated strategies that are designed to 'de-racialise' industry and some other areas of society. The effect of this is to divide off certain privileged members of Black society leaving workers at the bottom of the privilege pile;

— the concentration of workers in industry has also concentrated them in the great urban townships;

— the particular structure of the South African economy with its high degree of state involvement, price controls and heavy dependence on international markets has made it a very sensitive economy. As a consequence attempts to 'buy off' the major part of the working class will fail. It is more likely that as some readjustments of privilege are attempted that it will have to be workers that suffer through inflation and lack of basic commodities;

— the above factors and South Africa's international economic importance are likely to force capital into the political open and as a consequence develop a worker response;

— although capital can at present hide behind apartheid it is also the case that if workers organise widely enough they can get great support from the international labour movement. Also international public opinion has to be very carefully watched by capital because both international and South African capital are dependent on their links with the rest of the world.

These then are some of the important factors that are favourable to the development of a working class movement in South Africa. However, this does not mean that this will automatically happen. To understand this, we need to look at the present political environment more carefully to see both the present political tendencies and to establish why some active leadership role should be played by the unions and FOSATU in particular.

Workers need their own organisation to counter the growing power of capital and to further protect their own interests in the wider society. However, it is only workers who can build this organisation and in doing this they have to be clear on what they are doing.

As the numbers and importance of workers grows then all political movements have to try and win the loyalty of workers because they are such an important part of society. However, in relation to the particular requirements of worker organisation, mass parties and popular political organisations have definite limitations which have to be clearly understood by us.

We should distinguish between the international position and internal political activity. Internationally, it is clear that the ANC is the major force with sufficient presence and stature to be a serious challenge to the South African state and to secure the international condemnation of the present regime. To carry out this struggle is a difficult task because South Africa has many friends who are anxious to ensure that they can continue to benefit from her wealth. The fact that the ANC is also widely accepted internally also strengthens its credibility internationally.

However, this international presence of the ANC which is essential to a popular challenge to the present regime places certain strategic limitations on the ANC, namely:

— to reinforce its international position it has to claim credit for all forms of resistance, no matter what the political nature of such resistance. There is, therefore, a tendency to encourage undirected opportunistic political activity;

— it has to locate itself between the major international interests. To the major Western powers it has to appear as anti-racism but not as anti-capitalist. For the socialist East it has to be least neutral in the superpower struggle and certainly it could not appear to offer a serious socialist alternative to that of those countries as the response to Solidarity illustrates. These factors must seriously affect its relationship to workers;

— accordingly, the ANC retains its tradition of the 1950s and 1960s when because there was no serious alternative political path it rose to be a great populist liberation movement. To retain its very important international position it has to retain its political position as a popular mass movement. This clearly has implications for its important military activities.

Internally we also have to carefully examine what is happening politically. As a result of the state's complete inability to effect reform and the collapse of their Bantustan policy, they are again resorting to open repression. Since 1976 in particular this has given new life to popular resistance and once again the drive for unity against a repressive state has reaffirmed the political tradition of populism in South Africa. Various political and economic interests gather together in the popular front in the tradition of the ANC and the Congress Alliance.

In the present context all political activity, provided it is anti-state, is of equal status. In the overall resistance to this regime, this is not necessarily incorrect. In fact without such unity and widespread resistance it would not be possible by means of popular mass movements to seriously challenge the legitimacy of the present regime.

However, the really essential question is how worker organisation relates to this wider political struggle. I have argued above that the objective political and economic conditions facing workers is now markedly different to that of 20 years ago.

Yet there does not seem to be clarity on this within the present union movement. There are good reasons for this lack of clarity.

As a result of repression most worker leadership is relatively inexperienced and this is made worse by the fact that their unions are weak and unstable organisationally. The union struggles fought against capital have mostly been against isolated companies so that the wider struggle against capital at an industry or national level have not been experienced. This also means that workers and their leadership have not experienced the strength of large-scale worker organisation nor the amount of effort required to build and democratise such large-scale organisation. Again state repression and the wider political activity reinforce previous experience where the major function of workers was to reinforce and contribute to the popular struggle.

Politically, therefore, most unions and their leadership lack confidence as a worker leadership, they see their role as part of wider struggle but are unclear on what is required for the worker struggle. Generally, the question of building an effective worker organisation is not dealt with and political energy is spend in establishing unity across a wide front.

However, such a position is clearly a great strategic error that will weaken if not destroy worker organisation both now and in the future. All the great and successful popular movements have had as their aim the overthrow of oppressive — most often colonial — regimes. But these movements cannot and have not in themselves been able to deal with the particular and fundamental problem of workers. Their task is to remove regimes that are regarded as illegitimate and unacceptable by the majority.

It is, therefore, essential that workers must strive to build their own powerful and effective organisation even whilst they are part of the wider popular struggle. This organisation is necessary to protect and further worker interests and to ensure that the popular movement is not hijacked by elements who will in the end have no option but to turn against their worker supporters.

Broad and complicated matters have been covered and it is difficult to summarise them even further. However, I shall attempt to do so in order for us to try and examine the role that FOSATU can play in this struggle.

1. That worker resistance such as strike action helps build worker organisation but by itself it does not mean that there is a working class movement.
2. There has not been and is not a working class movement in South Africa.
3. The dominant political tradition in South Africa is that of the popular struggle against an oppressive, racist minority regime.
4. That this tradition is reasserting itself in the present upsurge of political activity.
5. However, the nature of economic development in South Africa has brutally and rapidly created a large industrial proletriat.
6. That the size and development of this working class is only matched by its mirror image which is the dramatic growth and transformation of industrial capital.
7. That before it is too late workers must strive to form their own powerful and effective organisation within the wider popular struggle.

FOSATU's objective

From what has been said we believe that FOSATU must set itself the task of giving leadership and direction to the building of a working class movement. Our efforts so far have equipped us to do this. Our organisation is nationally based, located in the major industries and the militancy of our members has generally developed a politically aware and self-critical leadership.

FOSATU as a trade union federation will clearly not constitute the working class movement nor would this place FOSATU in opposition to the wider political struggle or its major liberation movement.

FOSATU's task will be to build the effective organisational base for workers to play a major political role as workers. Our task will be to create an identity, confidence and political presence for worker organisation. The conditions are favourable for this task and its necessity is absolute.

We need have no fear of critics — our task will contribute to the wider liberation struggle and will also ensure that the worker majority is able to protect and further its interests. Ours is a fundamental political task and those who ask of workers their political support without allowing them the right to build their own organisation must answer for *their* real motives.

As was said above, capital has transformed itself and has a greater capacity to tolerate worker organisation because it is now more powerful and better able to deal with a worker challenge. Also because of its absolutely central position it will have the full support of the state in its actions and in the bitter struggles that are to come.

This requires a very much greater effort to establish worker organisation and requires thorough organisational work and ceaseless mobilisation of our members. The growth and transformation of capital has created the very preconditions for large-scale worker organisation.

Our concrete tasks and challenges

If we set the above as our general direction then we must deal with concrete tasks and challenges.

Organisation

What is crucial in organisation is the quality of the organisation — the quality that gives it its overall political direction and capability. As is clear from the experience of the advanced industrial countries that we looked at earlier, organisational size alone is not enough, yet without size there can be no effective counter to capital.

Broadly one can distinguish three factors that affect the quality of worker organisation — the structure of organisational strength and decision making; the location of organisational strength and the political qualities of its leadership structures.

Structure

The structure of an organisation should be such that it correctly locates worker strength and makes best use of that strength.

FOSATU's experience in this has been very important. Our organisation is built up from the factory floor. As a result, the base of the organisation is located where workers have most power and authority and that it where production takes place. This also has the effect of democratising our structures since worker representatives always participate from a position of strength and authority in the organisation. By stressing factory bargaining we involve our Shop Stewards in central activities and through this they gain experience as worker leadership. It should be said that they do battle every day.

These factory-based structures are the key to transforming pure quantity of members into a flexible and effective quality. Capital's hostility to factory organisation forces members and Shop Stewards to struggle continuously or else to have their organisation crushed.

At the union level FOSATU has attempted to build broad industrial unions on a national basis. We, in effect, have a position of one affiliate per industry. We have chosen industrial unions because of the organisational advantages we gain in our struggle against capital. However, FOSATU's role is to link these industrial unions into a tight federation that is based on common policy and a sharing of resources. Our aim is to keep a unity of purpose among affiliates at all levels of their organisation.

Our task in the three years to come must be to consolidate and develop factory organisation, a national presence for our unions and to reassert unity of purpose among affiliates.

The structures we are developing are an essential basis for effective and democratic organisation and are the basis for greater worker participation in and control over production.

Location

The question of location is closely related to structure. Without correct structures then the location of one's organisational strength is not as important.

We must accept that it will take many years to organise all workers and at present that should not be our aim. Our present aim must be to locate our organisation strategically. We need to look at the location of our organisational strength in relation to the industry, geographic area and the points at which we can most effectively carry out collective bargaining.

Our major affiliates should be located in the major industries. Within those industries we must become a substantial presence by carefully building our organisation in major factories, companies and areas.

Geographically we must clearly aim to be a national presence both as FOSATU and as the affiliates. Our organisation should be able to dominate major industrial areas. By doing this we create the major means whereby worker organisation can play a significant if not dominant role in the communities that surround these industrial areas.

Successful collective bargaining requires that the organisation is capable of mobilising its members behind demands. Thus far our unions have only really been able to mobilise at the plant level. However, the experience of NAAWU which is exceptional in FOSATU has shown what can be gained by mobilising across companies. We have flexible structures and we must use them if we are to serve our members. We must be able to mobilise across factories and in local areas across industries. We must see industry bargaining or regional bargaining not as something to be feared but as the logical extension of our present structures and practices.

Worker leadership

Here we must be immediately clear that we are not talking about leadership in the sense that it is usually discussed — which is in terms of individuals and 'great men'. This view of leadership is not what is important for a worker organisation. What we are interested in is the elected representatives of workers and the officials they appoint to work within the organisation.

We are interested in how the leadership is elected or appointed; who it is answerable to and how this accountability is achieved; how experienced leadership is and how it gains this experience and how they develop means of training and educating leadership so that it remains self-critical and politically active.

The challanges facing worker leadership are undoubtedly different to other leadership groups. For worker leadership in a capitalist society, your everyday struggle is related to your job and therefore your wage and therefore your very ability to survive. The most appropriate comparison is with that of the guerrilla fighter who has to develop the strength to resist daily, the knowledge of his terrain that will give him every tactical advantage and the support of those for whom he is struggling. Probably most important because both the worker leader and the guerrilla are fighting a powerful enemy, is the development of a sense of when to advance and when to retreat.

These skills are not easily learnt and not easily replaced. So worker leadership cannot be wasted by opportunistic and overly adventuristic actions.

We are also concerned with worker leadership in a wider arena than only that of the union struggle. Giving leadership to the working class requires an organisational base. Without this base, then the poverty and the lack of education, information and time that workers are struggling against will be the very factors which will force workers to surrender leadership of the community to other strata in society.

Our aim is to use the strength of factory-based organisation to allow workers to play an effective role in the community. Worker leadership will have:

— gained invaluable political experience from their factory struggles;
— organisation and resources behind them;
— organisational structures and location that will give them localised strength;
— the ability to speak with a clear and democratically established worker mandate.

The points made here should be our guide for action and we have a long way to go in building a larger leadership structure that has the political qualities of clarity, determination, discipline and the ability to be self-critical.

Working class identity

The task of organisation outlined above and more important, the quality of that organisation will absorb most of our energies in the next three years, and is, therefore, our major priority. Yet to give leadership in the building of a working class movement we must start to build a greater identity for worker organisation.

In a very important way the building of effective trade unions does create a worker identity. However, there is the danger that the unions become preoccupied with their members and ignore workers generally. By establishing a clear political direction we can avoid this.

One answer that is often proposed is to be involved in community activities. That FOSATU should be involved in community activities is correct since our members form the major part of those communities. However, as we have argued above we must do so from an organisational base if we are truly to be an effective worker presence.

Without this base, it is more likely that we will destroy a clear worker identity since workers will be entirely swamped by the powerful tradition of popular politics that we examined earlier.

It is also the case that there has emerged into our political debate an empty and misleading political category called 'the community'. All communities are composed of different interest groups and for a worker organisation to ally itself with every community group or action would be suicide for worker organisation. Under the surface of unity community politics is partisan and divided. FOSATU cannot possibly ally itself to all the political groups that are contesting this arena. Neither can it ally itself with particular groups. Both paths will destroy the unity of its own worker organisation.

This simple political fact is the reason for one of our founding resolutions. It has nothing to do with not wanting to be involved in politics. Our whole existence is political and we welcome that. Our concern is with the very essence of politics and that is the relation between the major classes in South Africa being capital and labour.

We need to state this more clearly and understand it ourselves more clearly. There is also no doubt that we must take our own newspaper very much more seriously as it can be a major instrument in building a worker identity.

At the level of organisation we have a sound base on which to work. Probably our main problem has been that we did not clearly state why we had chosen certain structures and what could be achieved by them.

As our political clarity and confidence grows, so we must state our position more clearly in our meetings, among our members and through our own newspaper.

Unity in the Labour Movement

Our first step must be to address ourselves to unity in the labour movement. If we are to create a working class movement then trade union unity has to be dealt with very early on in our struggle. Because we take working class politics seriously we must take trade union unity seriously.

At present there is a very great momentum to unity in the labour movement and we have to carefully consider and analyse what is happening.

The first point to understand is that all the unions involved in the talks are relatively weak in relation to their potential — some appallingly so. Many are too easily fooled by their own propaganda and the great interest shown by everyone into believing that they are now a strong force.

Furthermore, with a few exceptions (mostly in FOSATU), these unions are not yet a national or an industrial presence. Their strengths lie in isolated factories and very few have any real geographic concentration. As a result, both the leadership of these unions and their membership have no clear conception of the organised power of capital nor for that matter of its weakness. There is no real experience of the difficulties of large-scale worker organisation nor of the difficulties in building democratic worker structures. The bulk of the present leadership has no clear conception of the needs of worker struggle or of a worker dominated society. There is all too often a contradiction between the political position and organisational practice. Radical political positions are adopted but the organisational practice makes little headway into the power of capital nor is it effectively democratic. A number of factors result from this — often capital is attacked in the 'abstract' by making it all powerful and accordingly seeing an attack on the state as the only answer, or political energies are spend in widespread campaigns. Actual worker organisation and advance is left weak and based on sporadic upsurges rather than on organisational strength.

As a consequence of these factors it is not possible for people to draw any distinction between worker struggle and popular struggle let alone understand the relation between the two in South Africa. The unity talks are therefore conceived of as being within the wider popular struggle and as another area where anti-state unity can be achieved. A formal unity rather than a working unity against capital is therefore seen as the prime object.

There are broadly speaking three forms of unity to the union movement at present and we should look at each fairly carefully:

Ad hoc unity: this is what has occurred at present where unity is issue-located and there are attempts to take a common stand. At present this unity is significant in that it creates unity out of apparent disunity. However, its significance will rapidly decline. Such *ad hoc* unity can only achieve anything on specific issues and it is inevitably forced to take more and more concerted and concrete actions unless it merely wants to be the source of endless press statements. Such further actions require a more permanent organisational link.

United front unity: here the organisations remain autonomous but they set up a permanent platform of contact. Some people seem to see the solidarity committees as such as platform. However, although this provides a more definite organisational link, considerable new problems are posed. Again the movement is towards more and more significant gestures of protest and the problem now posed is how are decisions to be taken and on what mandate. Does each organisation have an equal vote or is voting by size? If decisions are on a consensus basis — then on what mandate? Should each organisation get a formal mandate on each issue and if they don't, how representative of rank and file membership is each decision? Is there not a greater than usual danger of decisions being taken by a few officials who have easy access to the meetings?

A permanent organisational link requires a process for making decisions that is democratic and equitable. Furthermore, if solidarity actions are to be successful they require organisational co-ordination — this in turn requires the power to sanction. How can this be done if participants are entirely autonomous?

A further step in this type of unity can be a 'loose federation' such as TUCSA, where the unions are now all in the same federal organisation and the symbolism of unity is far greater. However, such a federal body — not being based on any clear principles — is unlikely to generate working unity as it would contend with numerous problems of jurisdiction between unions and it is unlikely that organisational rationalisation could take place without firm policies and particular structures.

In fact 'United front unity', with or without a loose federation, can destroy the hope of greater unity by creating unresolved differences and no acceptable way of resolving these.

Disciplined unity: this requires common political purpose, binding policy on affiliates and close working links based on specific organisational structures.

If such a federation is based on industrial unions then FOSATU is the closest to being an example of such 'undisciplined unity' — in the present circumstances.

If the federation were not based on an industrial structure but on a regional one, then it is more difficult to set out its working structures since there is no clear experience of how this would work. However, there is no doubt that some allowance would have to be made for industrial considerations and the industrial organisation of capital. In FOSATU we have argued that industrial unions in a 'tight federation' allow for maximum flexibility and efficacy.

It is clear from this that unity means little unless these factors are taken into account. To talk lightly of unity is to keep it within the framework of

ad hoc or united front unity. The effectiveness of such unity would rapidly disappear. So if that is what is meant by unity we have to imply certain possible motives of its proponents:
— inexperience and lack of thought on the matter;
— political expediency whereby this unity is for specific limited ends of embarrassing certain organislations;
— a preoccupation with popular politics and a lack of commitment to the building of a working class political position.

However, if we in FOSATU are to take our objective seriously and that objective is the building of a working class movement then we have to take unity very seriously. Clearly by unity we should strive for 'disciplined unity' since it is only such unity that can possibly meet our objective.

We must ourselves work out a programme for unity and on the basis of that programme we should not hesitate to attack those who are impeding the development of a working class movement.

Conclusion

The issues that have been covered in this paper are important and complicated — they are the basis for an understanding of the true nature of the workers struggle in South Africa and the political role our organisation must play in that struggle.

We believe that in FOSATU we have a firm base on which to build organisationally. Our task in the three years to come is to firmly commit ourselves to a working class political position. With this greater political understanding we must:
— consolidate our organisational structures;
— give guidance and leadership in the building of a larger working class movement in South Africa;
— seek out comrades and allies who will join us in this struggle;
— and in this way make our fundamental contribution to the liberation of the oppressed people of South Africa.

In doing this we must all be clear that we shall never be so petty as to insist on our organisation's name as the only one in the trade union movement which can carry out this task. It is what the organisation does that is important — not what it is called. Yet equally, we shall never be so politically foolish as to abandon the worker struggle.

Appendix 2

The General Workers' Union on the United Democratic Front

In November 1983, the *South African Labour Bulletin* (SALB) published a series of interviews and statements about the relationship of the emerging trade unions with the black political groupings in South Africa, in particular, the United Democratic Front (UDF).

To begin with SALB interviewed the General Workers' Union on its attitude to the United Democratic Front. The following preamble from the GWU explains the context in which it felt it necessary to clarify its views publicly. The preamble is followed by the interview.

Amidst the controversy surrounding the position of many unions with regard to the UDF, the GWU feels that it is important that our position and views on this issue are clear. In addition, we believe that debate of this nature is healthy within and between progressive organisations.

This controversy has involved much criticism. We do not see criticism as necessarily negative. Some criticism may be based on a detailed understanding of, and disagreement with, our reasons for not affiliating to the UDF. This merely reflects the fact that, quite predictably, different outlooks on political issues do exist within the democratic movement. Some criticism has, however, been based on a distortion of our position. Perhaps this is due in part to the fact that there has not been enough detailed publication of our reasons for not affiliating to the UDF.

We take issue with claims and resulting criticisms that we do not support the UDF or that we are 'not interested in politics'. The interview with our General Secretary answers these allegations in detail. We stress again what we have repeatedly and publicly stated: that we support any organisation opposing the new constitution and other laws which deny the majority of South Africans democracy. Our support obviously extends to the UDF. We have stated our willingness to participate jointly in campaigns and give our general support in a variety of ways.

Neither do we say 'we will never join the UDF', a view attributed to us in some reports. We do have real difficulties, however, and explain these, in affiliating as a single workers' organisation to the UDF. One possible scenario for the future mentioned in the interview is that of a national union federation affiliating to a national political body. It must be emphasised once again however, that we are an organisation which acts on mandates from our membership. As such, this kind of unity would have to be one called for by the rank-and-file members. As stated in the interview, a national union federation may provide workers with the necessary support to participate in a multi-class organisation. Participation of workers on the ground rather than through an alliance merely 'at the top' would still be imperative.

We put our views forward in the hope of clarifying the present misunderstanding and encouraging discussion.

Why has the General Workers Union decided not to affiliate to the United Democratic Front?

The first point, which we've stated repeatedly, is that we are committed to supporting any organisation which opposes the constitutional proposals and the Koornhof Bills, and the UDF would obviously be primary amongst those organisations. We are also committed to the idea of joint campaigns with the UDF in opposing the Bills and the constitution. But we don't see our way clear to affiliating to the UDF. Our difficulties there relate to two broad areas, two broad issues. The first concerns the structure of many of the other organisations that are affiliated to the UDF, relative to the structure of a trade union. These structures are very distinct and critically different. Our second major area of difficulty relates to the essentially single class nature, working class nature of trade unions, relative to the multi-class nature of the UDF, and of many of the organisations affiliated to the UDF.

What do you see as the essential differences in structure between the General Workers Union and other trade unions, on the one hand, and many of the organisations affiliated to the UDF, and why do you think those differences present obstacles to affiliation to the same organisation?

The answer to that question is long and complicated. It's relatively simple, difficult as that has proved to be in practice, for one union to affiliate to another union, because trade unions to all intents and purposes have identical structures. They all have factory structures, branch structures, and national structures, so that one union can fairly easily lock into another union at all levels of both organisations. This is simply not the case with a great many of the UDF. To take two concrete examples from the Western Cape: the Ecumenical Action Group called TEAM, and the Detainees Parents Support Committee. The former is a grouping of progressive priests, and the latter is a grouping of individuals dedicated to opposing detention, and providing support for those in detention. Let me be clear from the outset that both of these are laudable and necessary ventures, but neither bear any similarity whatsoever to the structure of a union. The same can be said in varying degrees of a great number of other organisations affiliated to the UDF, all the youth and student bodies, for example. The critical feature that all these organisations have in common, as far as we can see, is that they are primarily organisations of activists. To say they are organsations of activists is not intended as a slight in any way, and we believe that there is a great need for this type of organisation in South Africa. But we still insist that they bear no similarity in their structure or organisational practice to a trade union. This problem has been recognised by the UDF, in the Western Cape, where some organisations, referred to as mass-based organisations, have been given a certain number of delegates. Other organisations, those that we would primarily refer to as activist organisations, have been given a smaller number of delegates. While this recognises that differences do exist, we believe that it is an inadequate recognition. The difference between an activist organisation and a mass-based organisation is not one of size, and therefore of the number of delegates to a central body, but rather of the entire structure and functioning of the organisation.

As we see it, an activist organisation is essentially a grouping of like-minded individuals, who are brought together by a common political goal. Their activity consists in propagating their ideas amongst a constituency which they themselves define. Activists grouped together in this way, in an organisation of this sort, have a great deal of freedom of manoeuvre in the extremely flexible parameters in which they operate. They don't represent members in a strong sense. They propagate ideas amongst a certain constituency, or in a certain area, and as such play a very important political role. Unions, on the other hand, are not organisations of activists, and union leaders are not activists in the same sense at all, because they are representatives in the strongest sense. Union leaders don't claim to represent the views of the working class. They represent the views of their members. Church or student activists, can claim to represent the broader social aspirations of church congregations or student bodies and it doesn't really matter whether they are actually mandated by the broad mass of students or churchgoers, or whether they are not. By propagating their ideas or their line they attempt to make students or churchgoers aware of their broader interests and their social role. A union leader, on the other hand, can't go to a factory and claim to speak for the working class. He has to be mandated by workers in a factory, and he has to be reasonably sure that the particular workers who have mandated him back up his mandate. In a union situation there is no alternative to working that way.

The critical upshot of this is that a union representative has to go through a long and very arduous process of receiving mandates and constantly ensuring that the mandates are backed. Union leaders don't derive their position from discussing ideas from amongst a small group of comrades, and then propagating these ideas widely. They derive their position from the members whom they've organised, and who send them forward with a specific mandate. Unquestionably union leaders can influence the mandate that is given by discussing issues with the rank and file, but ultimately they are very tightly bound to the specific decisions of members. This is, as far as we see, what a mass-based organisation means. It's got nothing to do with the size of the organisation, its got to do with the difference between organisational politics and activist politics. The structure of a union derives from the relationship between the shop steward committee and the members in a particular factory. It is undoubtedly at that level where the mandated relationship is the strongest, but it works in that way all the way up to the top of the organisation, all the way up to the national conference, and we cannot, change our hats to suit different occasions, and still retain our character as representative organisations. We have to go through the process of getting these mandates, we have to know that our members are willing to back the mandates and what they are willing to do. If we don't do that our participation is either meaningless, or even worse than that, our participation could be construed by our members as being in violation of the most basic trade union principle, namely the principle of representivity. Those considerations simply don't apply to a large number of the organisations affiliated to the UDF. Most of the organisations affiliated to the UDF have as their legitimate political task, to appeal to the masses 'out there'. We have as our task the representation of the workers inside our organisation, and the painstaking process of drawing more and more members into the formal and disciplined structure of a trade union. This is a major reason why we've found it difficult to envisage fitting into the structure of the UDF. We've experienced huge difficulty in explaining to our members how we would fit into the UDF as a union, yet conversely we have found it very easy to explain to our members how we would fit into a trade union federation. The difficulties that we have don't arise from the issues which the UDF has been set up to tackle. These have been discussed in the union, and they are very broadly appreciated. But affiliation has aroused very little interest.

There's one additional point that I want to emphasise. We've stated repeatedly that we'll encourage our members to join the UDF. Well, given the federation structure of the UDF, that's impossible, but we'll encourage our members to join organisations that are affiliated to the UDF. Should one of our members rise to become even a leader of the UDF, we would not view that as inconsistent with union policy in the slightest. In fact it would probably be a source of great pride to the union, just as it's a source of great pride to us whenever any of our members become leaders in their progressive community organisations. But we do not see our way clear to representing our members as a union in the UDF.

Your referred earlier to problems in the relationship between the union as a single class organisation, and other organisations affiliated to the UDF which are multi-class organisations. Could you elaborate on that?

It's not even primarily a question that the union is a single-class organisation, but that the union is a working class organisation, and a working class organisation only. A union by definition is open to workers only. This is not to say that there are never divisions in a trade union. There obviously are. There are a group of people in a trade union who are not workers, namely all the full-time officials, and their interests have always to be subordinated to the interests of the members. There are also divisions within a union on the basis of the skill categorisation of workers in a factory. In South Africa there are also the inevitable racial differences and potential divisions between section 10 people and contract people. It's these divisions which the constitution and the Koornhof Bills have been set up to widen. They are divisions that we always have to work on, that we always have to work at overcoming. But notwithstanding these divisions, all our members are working class. They are all factory members, and they are all members of the broader society. This means that they identify, quite correctly, as their source of oppression, the bosses and the state. That has bearing on the question of our affiliation to the UDF. For one thing, we will inevitably be an organisation that incorporates a great diversity of political views and affiliations. We'll have within our ranks members with militant political views, and we'll have in our ranks members with fairly conservative political views. We'll also have within our ranks a great many members who have few political views at all, people who have joined the organisation purely to fight their bosses. With a certain degree of tension now and again, those diverse views can all be contained within an organisation, because they are all held by workers.

To a certain extent this could also be said of any other mass-based organisation. It could be said of student organsations where these are mass-based, it could be said of womens' organisations where they are mass-based, it could be said even of a community organisation. It is conceivable that a woman joins a womens' organisation to fight womens' issues. Such an organisation should be able to contain within it a fair diversity of general political views as well. But there are two key differences. The first is that student and community organisations, and, although not necessarily correctly, women's organisations, tend to identify the state as their source of oppression. This means that they are inevitably more clearly politically defined, and their membership is more clearly a politically based membership. They don't have the bosses to intercede in the struggle in the same way that workers in a trade union do. Secondly, the fact of the matter is that in South Africa, most non-trade union progressive organisations, tend to identify themselves quite strongly with one or another political tendency.

This of course involves particular problems in Cape Town. I don't know if these problems are the same everywhere else. But here the community organisations are divided quite clearly into two groups. There was a possibility that affiliation could jeopardise the unity of, if not directly our union in Cape Town, certainly of some other unions in Cape Town. This is also especially sensitive when we've identified as a priority the formation of a trade union federation, with the even greater diversity of views that are contained therein. Just as we wouldn't want to do anything that would jeopardise the unity of the whole trade union movement. I'm aware that opens us up to what has become a currently fashionable charge, namely that we are economistic. Although it's not always clear from those levelling the accusation, I take this to mean that we concentrate our activities exclusively on wages and working conditions, that we're not concerned with political struggle, that the only basis of our unity is the struggle in the factory. It's as such, a unity that makes little positive contribution to the national democratic struggle. There are two answers to this: the first is that a union must inevitably carry within it the tendency towards economism. A factory-based organisation by definition sets itself certain limits, and the General Workers Union has never made any claim to mystically transcend these limits. The second answer to the question is that the accusation reflects a very narrow, formalistic notion of what politics is, and that's what really brings us to a point pertinent to the question of the class composition of the union. It has to be acknowledged that workers are a very special group in the society. They are the class, unfashionable that term might be, that produces the wealth of the country. As such they are the most exploited and oppressed members of society. This special place of the workers in society is currently recognised in a very peculiar and inverse way by other groups in society. The way in which it's recognised in South Africa is by frantic attempts by other groupings to eliminate the differences between themselves and the working class. What you have ranges from the laughable assertion made some years ago to the effect that all blacks are workers, to more serious assertions made by community leaders and very often trade union leaders today, to the effect that the community are the workers and the workers are the community, or student activists who are the workers of tomorrow, or women's organisations who are the wives and daughters of the workers. All these assertions have a kernel of truth, but to be a worker of tomorrow is not to be a worker of today.

More pertinently it doesn't go any way towards transforming a student organisation into a workers' organisation. To say that workers constitute the majority of any black community in South Africa is obviously true, but it doesn't mean that workers constitute the majority of community organisation, of organised community organisation, of organised community members. In fact, it's lamentable, but nonetheless true, that community organisations have had relatively little insertion into the ranks of contract workers, for example. In those rare cases where the majority of a particular community organisation are in fact working class people, its possible that these working class members will have little influence at the top of the organisation in the decision making structures of the organisation.

I want to be clear about one thing: when we say that workers are the most oppressed and exploited members of society, that means, at the general level, that workers do not have access to the means of production, and that, to be workers, they have to be deprived of the possibility of turning themselves into bosses. This, even at that general level, is not necessarily true of other groups in society. It's not for example necessarily true of students. But what it means at a more specific level, a level more specific to our problems with affiliation to the UDF, to a multi-class organisation, is that workers as a class are necessarily denied access to skills and education, other than those that are directly required by the bosses in production. They are denied the skills of articulation and language, of literacy, numeracy, in fact of the whole culture and short hand which a smoothly functioning organisation seems to require. This is not to mention the fact that workers also have very little time at their disposal, or at any rate the time at the disposal of the workers is very rigidly controlled. It is in fact control that is key-defining element of what it means to be a member of the working class. Every minute of a worker's time is controlled, he's told when and how and where he'll work, he's told when and where and how he'll sleep, he has no control over whether he is employed one day and unemployed the next day. All workers have, in a sense, is their unity. This is why workers tend so naturally to take and implement decisions *en masse,* and conversely why other groupings in society are so comfortable with taking decisions individually or in small groups, even, which is very characteristic of student organisations, to break up large gatherings into small groups to facilitate decision making and discussion.

The point of this digression isn't to say that workers should never co-operate, never work together with organisations of non-workers, or organisations in which non-workers are also members. We would expect this of our members. But we wouldn't be surprised, and nobody else should be surprised, if when our members do work in this way, they insist on carrying into these organisations the culture and demands of the working class, and the culture and demands of a working class organisation. Because, and this is where I really do want to answer the charge of economism to some extent, unquestionably the democratic union movement in South Africa has won substantial economic gains, and to be sure we've spent a major part of our time and energy in making these economic gains. But in the democratic unions, the workers have also in addition won a new pride and dignity, a self-confidence in their ability to take and implement decisions. This is really the key aspect of unions' political work. The acquisition by our members of an awareness of their own power, an awareness of their ability to participate in their own way in the most complex and difficult decisions. We don't claim for one minute that this should or does represent the totality of our political work. Nor do we make the claim that this is sufficient to democratise South Africa. But we are absolutely certain that the level of organisation of workers in South Africa has reached a stage where they simply won't settle for any less than the right to participate fully in any political or community organisations that they form, or that they join. This is especially so if they join these organisations in their capacities as union members. They won't be satisfied with formal symbols of power, nor will they be satisfied with power where the ability to exercise that power resides with the more skilled and educated union bureaucrats, where they become in a sense silent but nevertheless muscular participants in the whole process.

We don't here want to get into a detailed critique of the UDF as such. But the UDF has to ask itself whether its style and tone, whether the language spoken, whether the pace at which it's developed, whether its programme, facilitate the fullest participation by working class people. Our members simply do not feel that way. They've never, for example, appreciated the need for the sophisticated structures which the UDF have introduced. This is not because they are backward or stupid, but because they are advanced leaders of their own organisation, an organisation which has been in existence for 10 years. We've never in the 10 years of our existence found the need to set up single sub-committees, let along a highly sophisticated and complex structure. The workers have not felt that they've had the time to participate in the endless debate surrounding the setting up of the UDF. This is not because they are uninterested in politics, but because they do arduous full-time jobs and they believe, unlike activists generally, that meetings are only necessary when the meetings have a very clear and defined objective, and when there's the possibility of that objective being fulfilled at the meeting.

We encouraged, for example, our members to attend the launching of the UDF. A fair number attended, but the vast majority of those who attended didn't understand the meeting, because it was in English. Principally the workers don't understand what programme of action is envisaged by the UDF, and this is obviously very critical. Given the above, there is a feeling on the part of the workers that they will not be able to participate fully in the decisions that lead to a programme of action, and this is anathema to an organised worker. They are not going to be drawn into an organisation in which they feel that they will have to take action blindly, without having participated in the decision making. Those are really the key aspects of the class composition of the organisations: firstly, that we draw in our membership from a very wide and diverse range of political views, unlike most of the other organisations participating in the UDF, and secondly, that our members are working class people, and as working class they come from a culture that is very distinct from that of other more privileged members of society.

There has been a lot of talk about the importance of working class leadership in national political organisation. Are you saying that working class leadership does not amount to the presence of individual members of the working class within national politically oriented organisations, but rather that the working class should have a leading status, within national political organisations?

I think that I mean both. It is essential that working class individuals occupy leading positions in national political organisations, inside the country. It's important because I believe the second to be true as well, that workers must have a special status in multi-class organisations. Workers must have the opportunity to lead the pace and style and tone and language — in fact the whole discourse — of the organisation. The reason why it's important, and the reason why I think that it's important to examine the questions raised with respect to the UDF, is that democracy in this country is inconceivable without the fullest struggle. This is not merely because the working class is the largest and most muscular group in society. Simply put, they are the only social grouping with a class interest in democracy. Other social classes or social groupings might have an interest in relative or partial democratisation of society; other individuals might have a moral interest in a thorough going democratisation of society. But the working class which has every aspect of it's life — its economic life and its political life, very rigidly controlled, is the one class in society that has an interest in a thorough going democratisation of the economy and the polity. Working class organisation in South Africa has developed to the stage where workers insist on the right to participate fully, in the structures of any organisation of which they are members.

The participation of Western Cape trade unions in the Disorderly Bills Action Committee (DBAC) last year, seemed to be an unsatisfactory experience, not only for the trade unions, but for the other organisations participating in the DBAC. Very little was achieved after a long series of meetings. To what extent do you think this has discouraged workers and trade unions in the Western Cape from participating in the UDF, which is seen as some bigger form of the DBAC.

In the initial stages of the formation of the UDF, our experience of the DBAC definitely did influence our feelings about participating in the UDF. The experiences on the DBAC were uniformly negative, in the sense that we found ourselves in the middle of extraordinary squabbles. Sometimes they seemed to be squabbles based on straight power plays, straight questions of dominance between the two factions of the community organisation in Cape Town. The upshot of that was nothing got done, with respect to the Koornhof Bills. I recall a laughable situation on one occasion — I myself wasn't present there, but our representatives reported — where in the same week that the Koornhof Bills were withdrawn, the DBAC met. They sat through an entire three- or four-hour meeting without once mentioning the Koornhof Bills. The DBAC seemed to be set up for some other purpose altogether. The purpose seemed to be one grouping in the community to achieve domination over another grouping in the community. This did colour our participation in the UDF at first, but it doesn't any more. We, like I imagine other groups who were equally disappointed with their experience of the DBAC, have shaken off the ill effect of that experience. Where it does still colour our decision is that particularly some unions draw their membership from one of these groupings in the community, and there are sometimes members of other community groupings in the union. We would not wish these differences in the community to intercede in the unity of a trade union, both of the grouping of trade unions in the Western Cape, and also of particular individual trade unions.

You talked earlier about the fact that the General Workers' Union supports the development of other progressive organisations in the community, and that it encourages participation of General Workers' Union members in those organisations. In what concrete ways has the General Workers' Union supported the development of these organisations, and how does it aim to do so in future?

The primary way, in which we attempt to facilitate the development of broader community organisations is by taking up broader issues in our union. This we've always done, and we continue to do. The issue of the Koornhof Bills and the constitution has been very substantially discussed in the union right from the beginning, before many of the organisations that have been specifically set up to oppose the Bills were even conceived of. This is really the primary way in which we support other organisations.

We would also support them, and we've said this repeatedly, by encouraging our members to join these organisations. We've fairly consistently been asked to give our members to other organisations. Well, our answer to that is that our members are not locked in concentration camps, our members are in the community, in the townships. They must be organised, and we would certainly encourage them to join these organisations.

What is the union's current relationship with the United Democratic Front, and what possible future developments do you see?

On the question of our current relationship to the UDF, we definitely see a role for ourselves as a union relative to the UDF. We've said repeatedly that we are prepared to engage in joint campaigns with the UDF, and that we are prepared to support UDF campaigns. We hope to be informed of UDF activities, of UDF meetings, to enable us to encourage our members to go to these meetings. Both of a local or regional nature. We hope that we will receive UDF newsletters and information sheets and that we will be able to hand these out to our members. For example, in the very near future in Cape Town the UDF are holding a meeting to discuss what is going on in the Ciskei. We see what is going on in the Ciskei as critically important to us, obviously. We also see it as a critically important exposé of the constitutional proposals, and therefore legitimately within the UDF's ambit. We would certainly support them in that campaign.

As to the future, that's a little bit hypothetical at the moment, I can't ever envisage the General Workers Union affiliating to the UDF. Although obviously I can't speak for any other union, I can envisage a situation where a formal relationship develops between a national/political/community centre like the UDF, and a national trade union centre. I should say on that score that there is a precedent for this in South Africa, for a relationship between a national explicitly political based centre and a national trade union centre.

It's often been said by the unions that their priority is the formation of a federation, and that is the case. The reason why it's a priority, or the reason why that priority influences our decision with respect to the UDF, is not that we are spending so much time in forming a federation that we don't have time to devote any resources to affiliating to the UDF. Rather we see that as part of a national trade union centre, the workers would have the necessary support, the necessary base, from which to participate in a multi-class organisation. That is a possible development. Obviously it would be a highly complex development, and one that would require a broad agreement in the trade union movement. But certainly it's a possibility, it has been done before, I don't see why it shouldn't be done again.

Appendix 3

The Municipal and General Workers' Union on the United Democratic Front

The Municipal and General Workers' Union of South Africa's response to this issue must begin by outlining how we see the present political situation. This is because our decision to join the UDF was made as part of our response to certain political events. These events directly affected us both as a trade union, and as people who identify ourselves with the struggle for a free and just South Africa.

There are four main political issues that effect workers today. These four are:

a. The increasing push towards Bantustan independence for all the homelands — and therefore the forcing of Bantustan citizenship on all Black people.

b. The attempt. to push through new Pass Laws that will tighten up the control of all workers. The lives of all workers, but more especially contract workers, will become very difficult if this new law is passed.

c. The Community Council elections that will be held later on this month. This issue is linked to the problem of high rents, high electricity bills and high transport costs.

d. The 'New Deal' being pushed by the government in the forthcoming constitution. This issue must be seen as a part of the issues spoken of above. All four of these issues are linked. They are all part of the attempt to ensure that the Apartheid capitalist system can continue to exploit workers by continuing to oppress all black people. We will explain what we mean by this in more detail below. First we will look at why these four issues are so important to black workers.

Bantustan independence

All black workers are faced with the fact that they and their children are being forced to become citizens of one or other homeland. As these homelands become independent — the situation of the workers from that homeland deteriorates. They are no longer seen as citizens of South Africa but as foreigners coming into South Africa to get a job. The government has made it clear that it hopes to eventually have no more black citizens of South Africa. All black people will be foreigners who can come into South Africa to work if there are jobs for them. If there are no jobs then they will be sent to the homelands to starve.

The Bantustans are governed by people who are junior partners in the oppression of the black people of South Africa. These governments are there to make sure that the large numbers of unemployed and hungry people in the homelands are kept under control. These governments survive only because they are given money and guns by the Botha government.

They exist only to oppress the people, and to keep them from rising up against their oppression.

All black workers are faced with the threat of being sent off to rot in a homeland. All black workers must unite to say NO to these Bantustans.

The new pass laws

The pass laws have always been the way in which the government of South Africa has made it easy for the bosses to exploit black workers. The pass laws control the movements of black workers. These are the laws which make it possible for the government to get rid of any workers who are not needed in the urban areas. These are the laws that have made it possible for the government and the bosses to force black workers into jobs they would never choose to do — on the mines or the farms. But the problem is that the very high numbers of unemployed people and the starvation in the homelands has resulted in people defying the control of the pass laws and coming to town illegally to look for jobs. So the government has decided to tighten up the pass laws in order to make sure that people do not come to the urban areas unless they are needed by the bosses.

The government has also decided that the best way of doing this is to try and divide the workers. The people who have jobs and houses in the urban areas will be given a little more freedom — and all others will be booted out into the homelands. No rural people will be registered for jobs if there is an urban person who does not have work. Anyone who tries to defy these laws by coming to town illegally will face a large fine and/or a long period in jail. Anyone who gives accommodation to an illegal worker will also face a large fine/or a long period in jail. Any employer who hired an illegal worker (because he can pay the worker less money) will be fined R500,000. (This is because the government feels that the problem of control over all black workers is more important than the extra profit that a few bosses can make by employing 'illegals').

Even though the urban workers with housing will be given a bit more freedom, their situation is also uncertain. This is because they could lose their position as permanent urban workers and end up in a homeland. The only way forward is to resist the government's attempts to divide workers and unite against these new pass laws.

All black workers are oppressed and controlled by the pass laws. All black workers will be affected by these new pass laws. This is why we must all unite to say NO to the 'Orderly Movement and Settlement of Black Persons Bill'.

The Community Council Elections

The Community councils are another attempt to confuse people about who the enemy is. This is done by putting stooges into power in the community councils and then oppressing the people through these stooges. When the Bantu Administration Boards were the people in charge, it was clear who the oppressor was. The UBCs had so little power that it was clear to everyone that they were the dummy bodies. The government then decided to give them a bit more power, change their name, and try to fool the people in this way. But the real power still lies in the hands of the government through the BAABs (Bantu Affairs Administration Boards).

This means that a whole lot of extra money is spent without any benefits for the people. These community councillors have to be paid high salaries, they need buildings to meet in, cars to ride around in — all in order to carry out the government's dirty work. The workers who live in the townships have to pay for all this. The government not only puts up stooges to do its dirty work for it — but it also tells the people that now that they control their own affairs — they will also have pay for it all by themselves — no more money from the government. This means that higher rents, higher electricity bills, dog tax and all sorts of other expenses will be forced upon the workers.

If the people complain, then the reply is that they are now in control of their own townships. They must complain to the people they elected. The government is also moving towards giving these councillors the power to oppress the urban people if they resist too much. Community guards — a type of police under the control of the community council — are being spoken about.

All black workers must unite to prevent the situation in the townships becoming like a mini-homeland. We must all unite to say NO to the community council elections.

The new constitution — no more apartheid?

Botha's 'New Deal' is being spoken about as a move away from Apartheid. The idea is that now Indian and Coloured people are being 'included', and that this is a step in the right direction. But if we look at this from the position of the black workers, we can see that this 'new deal' is just the same old apartheid — the same old oppression. The government is speaking of a new non-racial democracy coming about with this 'new deal'. This can only make sense if we first do away with all black people in South Africa. If there are no black South Africans (only Transkeians, Vendas, etc) then suddenly the whites are in the majority. Suddenly it becomes possible to include Coloureds and Indians in the government. So this 'so-called' move away from Apartheid is only possible thanks to the ultimate result of Apartheid — the banishing of all black South Africans to the Bantustans.

In this way we can see how this 'New Deal' is very closely linked to the other issues spoken of above: the 'Independence' of the Bantustans — the tightening up of the pass laws — and the new self-government of the townships. The government is hoping to win over the Coloured and Indian people in order to tighten up the oppression of the black people — and most especially — the black workers.

The 'New Deal' is trying to divide the oppressed people. This 'New Deal' is trying to make sure that the black workers remain under the control of the government. This 'New Deal' will make sure that the black workers are still at the mercy of the bosses.

All black workers and other oppressed people must unite to say NO to the whole package — the Constitution and the Koornhof Bills.

Who else is affected?

We have spoken of the way in which black workers are affected by this 'package deal'. We can see that the Apartheid capitalist system in our country is fighting to survive. The people are resisting and all sorts of problems are surfacing. This 'New Deal' — and the Koornhof Bills — are attempts by the government to face the challenges made by the people's resistance. We have seen how this tightening up of Apartheid laws will make it easier for the bosses to continue the exploitation of black workers. The government is passing these laws in order to make sure that the black working class is tightly controlled in the urban areas — and kicked out to the homelands when workers are no longer needed.

But these laws are also part of the Apartheid system that oppresses many people from other classes and other communities. All black people — and Indian and Coloured people — are oppressed by these laws. The black workers are the largest and most oppressed group. This is why black workers will usually be the most dedicated and hardworking people in the struggle. But black workers are not the only oppressed people. We must stand together with all people willing to fight for a free and just South Africa. We must unite to oppose this 'New Deal' and the Koornhof Bills. Only in this way can we mobilise the widest possible grouping of people to reject continued oppression.

We must recognise that within this broad unity of people — there will be differences of approach — different levels of understanding — different ideas about the kind of society we are fighting for. This does not matter. We are united in our opposition to Apartheid and its effects on all black people. The black workers will put all their might behind a thrust to do away with Apartheid and the injustices and inequalities that it has resulted in.

We believe that this cannot be done without a total change in the type of society that has been created by the Apartheid capitalist system in South Africa.

Trade Unions and the struggle

Our stand on these issues is clear — but how can we oppose them effectively? Trade Unions are not political parties. Trade Unions are organisations of workers — uniting to fight for the rights of workers and to defend these rights on the shop floor. Our Trade Unions are also committed to fighting for a society in which all workers are free. But we cannot pretend that all our members are politically-conscious people who would wholeheartedly get involved in the struggle. Our strength lies in our ability to unite in the workplaces with the possibility of stopping production. This happens mainly around some of the immediate problems facing workers in that workplace. The structures of our unions exist to enable workers to deal with problems in the workplace as they arise. Because union structures bring workers together to discuss problems — it becomes possible for political issues to be discussed. However, it is very difficult for a trade union to launch and control political campaigns — as well as function effectively as the first line of defence of the workers. This is why it is very difficult for us — as trade unions — to respond effectively to political issues. While admitting all this, we must say at the same time that it is our duty as trade unionists in South Africa to be part of the struggle for freedom and justice. Our problem is therefore to find the most effective way of doing this — despite the limitations of our organisations. This brings us to the need for alliances with other organisations.

Alliances

In South Africa, the main political organisations are banned. We are thus faced with finding ways of responding — together with other groupings of oppressed — to the main political struggles occurring inside our country. Many other organisations — like student groupings or community organsations — have a similar problem. They are formed to fight some of the basic problems that occur amongst people they are organising. They are not political parties. If they spent all their time functioning as political groupings — they would lose touch with their base.

Ordinary people have to be drawn into the process of struggle — they do not come rushing in by themselves. Ordinary people need to learn — through the process of struggling to change some of the immediate problems around them — how and why these immediate problems (like high rents, bad teaching, etc.) are part of broader political problems. In this sense, the difficulties these groups have in responding effectively to political issues are similar to those faced by the unions. This is why we have all responded so eagerly to the formation of the UDF.

The UDF and the crisis

Everybody today seems to be talking about the crisis. Well, the reality is that the present system of domination and exploitation is not working too well. So the government has a crisis on its hands. The 'New Deal' and the Koornhof Bills are the government's attempt to resolve this crisis by bringing in a shiny new model. This new model is supposed to make sure that the crisis becomes a thing of the past and that domination and exploitation live on . . . happily ever after. It's up to us to make sure that this does not happen.

This means that the present political situation demands a far greater and more united response than we have managed for a very long time. By ourselves — whether we are unions, community organisations, students or whatever — we will achieve very little. The present situation calls for the kind of united response that can bring together the strengths and talents of as many different groupings of people as possible. Churches, unions, community organisations, students, youth groups, women's groups and groups of activists — committees of all kinds — all of these should unite to resist this new 'package deal'.

The problem then becomes how to bring all these different types of organisations together. Herein lies the strength of an organisation like the UDF. In the real sense of the word — the UDF is not an organisation at all. It's a rallying point. It's the focus of a range of different types of energies. It represents the pooling of resources; the co-operation of a range of very different, autonomous organisations. It is a form of unity in action — but not in structure/form or detailed policy. It is an attempt to create the

POWER!

broadest possible unity in opposition to this specific political situation. It serves as a means of bringing people together. It serves as a forum to sort through the differences that may arise between the groupings — but only those differences that may serve as a stumbling block to this united opposition. All other differences are irrelevant to the project of the UDF.

The UDF also serves as a symbol of our determination to oppose oppression to the end. The election of presidents and patrons should be understood for their symbolic value — rather than as a set of very complicated structures. The individuals involved were chosen because they are symbols of our struggle — symbols of determination: of courage and of the history of our struggle. It is in all these ways that the UDF is a United Front of a broad range of organisations and not a unitary (or even a federal) structure.

As far as the operation of the UDF is concerned this means that the programmes of the UDF must be carried out primarily through the organisations that identify themselves with the UDF. The shared planning process, the pooling of resources and the employment of a number of full-time personnel by the UDF: all these things ensure that member organisations of the UDF receive a lot of support in the process of carrying out these programmes.

The most interesting result of the excitement and activity generated by the UDF so far, has been the emergence of a whole range of new organisations that then join the UDF. A number of youth organisations and civic organisations have emerged throughout the country to take up the UDF banner. These organisations exist as autonomous entities — although they have emerged as a result of the existence of the UDF. They will now be able to grow, consolidate their base, foster new leadership and continue to function long after the UDF ceases to exist. But what about unions? What kind of role should they play in the UDF?

Unions and the UDF

Unions are working class organisations. They exist both as a means to fight for the rights of workers — and as a training ground which enables workers to develop skills in organisation and leadership. The development of these skills — as well as the growing confidence that this generates amongst workers — are essential elements in the development of the working class struggle.

The main limitation of all unions is that their structure and way of operating tends to push them towards focusing only on economic issues — to the exclusion of political issues. This can only be overcome by associating ourselves — as a trade union — with the political struggles going on around us. In this way we can achieve two goals at the same time:

a. we can oppose the tendency towards economism by clearly stating our commitment — as trade unionists — to the broader struggle for freedom. This challenges all the workers that we organise to also examine their role in these terms; and

b. by actively participating in these struggles, we can influence their direction and goals. Worker leaders, emerging from the training ground of the unions, can take their places amongst the leadership of the political struggle. Workers — organised through the unions — can participate actively in the process of struggle. If this active participation occurs — the large number of workers involved will be a tremendous boost to the political struggle and will help to ensure that the aims of the struggle are controlled by the workers.

What alternatives do we have if we reject bodies like the UDF?

Some would argue that unions are working class bodies and in the interests of working class autonomy we must 'go it alone'. The unions should be part of an independent initiative against the 'new deal'. This independent opposition group should consist only of unions. Even if we felt this to be a good idea (which we don't) we would oppose it on the grounds that we spoke of above: a union is not a political organisation and for as long as it continues to function as a union — it cannot effectively fulfill the role of a political organisation. The other alternative would be for the unions to support/encourage the setting up of a 'Worker's Party' that will lead the workers in the struggle against the 'new deal'. This type of political grouping — it is argued — would ensure that the political goals of the working class are promoted. We disagree with this position for the following reasons:

a. No 'working class party' is ever composed only of workers. Anyone who is prepared to fight for the kind of fundamental changes that would enable workers to be free would be welcome in any working class party. This also points to the mistake of assuming that all workers are somehow automatically committed to the struggle for fundamental change. It is true that a progressive political direction can most naturally take root amongst the working class — it is not true that a political leadership composed of workers is automatically progressive. Nor is it true that a political leadership composed of workers will guarantee that the interests of the workers are promoted by that leadership.

   We believe that a truly fundamental change in this society can only occur if the workers are actively involved in the process of struggle. This is because the workers are one of the most down-trodden and oppressed classes in our society — as well as having a very important role in the functioning of our Apartheid capitalist society. This gives workers the kind of power that other oppressed classes — like the rural people (peasants) — do not have. The question then arises — In what way should workers be involved in the struggle? This leads us to the second objection that we have to the idea of a workers' party 'going it alone'.

b. We mentioned — in the first part of our discussion — the fact that it is the black workers of South Africa who have suffered most under the various parts of the Apartheid capitalist system. This is because this system functions in such a way as to enable the bosses to make the highest possible profits — at the expense of the workers. Many other people have also suffered terribly at the hands of this system — the rural poor people for example. It is because we believe that the oppression of black workers is at the roof of the broader oppression of all black people in South Africa — that we advocate the widest possible unity of all oppressed people to fight this system.

Some who will unite with us will not be prepared to go as far as we will on the road to freedom — but because it is the same road — we can unite and work together. Some believe that we will be betrayed by those who would get rid of racial discrimination but are not too keen to shake things up any further. Our reply to this is quite simple.

We believe that it is impossible to separate off Apartheid from the capitalist system it has fed. A truly committed opposition to Apartheid (and its consequences) will lay the foundations for a fundamental change in the entire system in South Africa. Our present struggle does not have to be based on some abstract 'ideal society' of the future. A struggle which aims to get rid of Apartheid — to get rid of the homelands — to get rid of the inequality bred by Apartheid, inequalities of wealth, land, education, etc. This kind of struggle — if taken to its logical conclusion — will undermine the foundations of Apartheid capitalism. The rest is up to us.

The importance of this kind of struggle is its ability to unite the widest possible range of oppressed people. The path of the struggle is the same for all of us — how far down the path we go will depend on our efforts. It's up to the unions and all other progressives to ensure that the organised workers are fully involved in the process of struggle — that worker leaders emerge and take up positions amongst the political leadership — that progressives unite to ensure a struggle for truly fundamental change in South Africa.

These are reasons for joining the UDF, we encourage all other progressives to do the same.

Appendix 4

The UDF on the Unions

The SALB (South African Labour Bulletin) interviewed Mr Mosiuoa Lekota, publicity secretary of the United Democratic Front, at Khotso House, Johannesburg on 13 December 1983.

What is a united democratic front?

It is an alliance of a wide spectrum of organisations: workers', youth, church, sporting organisations and so on. The UDF is an alliance specifically in opposition to the constitutional proposals and the Koornhof Bills. It is an umbrella body seeking to co-ordinate organisations previously acting independently.

Does this involve an alliance of different classes?

An alliance of classes is built into the United Democratic Front. For example workers' organisations and professional organisations contain different classes. But the United Democratic Front is essentially an alliance of organisations.

How was the UDF formed?

At the time when the Presidents' Council proposals and the Koornhof Bills were put forward opposition to them was coming from small, unco-ordinated organisations. At the anti-SAIC (Anti-South African Indian Council) meeting in Johannesburg in January Dr Boesak suggested that a united democratic front should be formed.

The call was well received and organisations represented at the meeting such as the Natal Indian Congress, the Joint Rent Action Committee and individuals who were members of the Cape Housing Action Committee contacted their members in other regions. The idea was passed on and mobilisation took place especially in Natal, the Transvaal and the Western Cape. In these areas UDF regions were being formed at meetings in April, May and June.

Further consultation led to the decision to launch the UDF nationally, even though not all the regions had been formed, because of the urgency of the situation. At the time of the national launch, on 20 August, the only fully structured regions were the Transvaal, Natal and the Cape. The other regions did their best but were not properly constituted.

Now we are organising in the North Western Cape, the Eastern Cape and Border region and the Free State. Apart from meetings being banned we are continuing to make strides in gaining support.

The UDF took nine months to form itself whereas the union movement has taken ten years to reach its present position. How do you account for this difference?

The UDF has organised organisations, it has not had to organise individuals in the same way as a trade union, which is more difficult and takes much longer. The strength of the UDF depends on the strength of the organisations which constitute it.

To what extent have you gained support amongst workers?

We are not satisfied that we have achieved as much trade union support as we had hoped for. But we see the participation of workers in the UDF as important. The more workers come in the closer we are to gaining a truly national character. South Africa is still under colonial conditions and the struggle against imperialism is a struggle against capitalism. For this reason the working class must provide the backbone of the struggle.

The question of sizes of organisations must be considered. For example professional organisations tend to be smaller than trade unions. In this regard organisations must receive representation proportionate to their strength in numbers.

What do you mean by 'a truly national character'?

We mean by this that we are non-racial, which means we embrace all races, and that we bring together all classes. The presence of workers and the middle classes in the UDF is well discernable, but a significant section of the working class in some major independent unions still remains outside our fold.

Do you feel, then, that whites have a contribution to make in the struggle?

Yes, for example students who were members of NUSAS (the National Union of South African Students) became stalwarts of the union movement.

Does your term 'national' also include all regions in South Africa?

Yes, by 'national' we mean all classes, all regions and all races.

To what extent does the UDF have a presence in the Bantustans?

We need a presence in these areas, but there the repression is worst. We have a strong presence in the Ciskei, but support for the UDF there is heavily suppressed.

Is your support in the Ciskei mainly through SAAWU (South African Allied Workers' Union)?

Yes, mainly through SAAWU but we have other support, as was shown by the numbers at the launching of the UDF in that region.

The Transkei is very different. Our supporters there can't express their support because they fear the consequences. In Zululand Gatcha (Buthelezi) claims that everyone belongs to Inkatha. It is difficult for anyone to show support for the UDF. But as support grows for the UDF in the urban areas amongst contract workers our message will be carried back to these areas.

What are the structures of the UDF?

The Transvaal region, for example, has a president, two secretaries, a treasurer and other executive members. Each region is affiliated to the national executive. The three regional presidents are also national presidents, but this is not a requirement, they just happen to have been elected to both positions. If an issue arises one of the two regional secretaries will call a regional general council. This is made up of delegates from the organisations affiliated to the UDF. The regional executive committee is elected by the regional general council. It does not include representatives from each affiliated organisation as this would make it too unwieldy. The executive committee runs the day-to-day affairs of the UDF.

In a few cases there are organisations which are national. Clause 5 of the UDF Working Principles provides for these organisations to affiliate nationally. The terms of their membership is decided by the national executive in consultation with the regional councils.

When an organisation has affiliated to the UDF it retains its independence. It cedes its independence only in regard to opposition to the constitutional proposals and the Koornhof Bills.

Could you briefly explain the UDF's programme of action?

We have set broad objectives, some activities may be possible in the Western Cape and others in the Transvaal. In the Transvaal, area committees are being established. There are to be workshops, door-to-door campaigns and mass meetings. The mass meetings give people a feeling of belonging together, but the door-to-door visits are the most important because people can ask questions. We are planning a peoples' weekend at the end of October at which there will be vigils focusing on the legislation. This will be part of the build-up to regional or provincial rallies on the eve of 2 November.

How do you see the role of the UDF differing from that of other organisations, particularly the unions?

The unions mainly handle the problems of working class people at the factory floor level. Some people have criticised unions for not taking up political issues, but the unions are not well equipped to handle political issues.

The members of trade unions can also participate in other organisations which take up other issues, for example the pass laws, bus fares, rents. Such issues require a different type of organisation.

Some unions, such as SAAWU, the Food and Canning Workers' Union, GWU (General Workers' Union) and others have taken up such issues in the past. With the emergence of the UDF do you see the role of these unions changing?

These unions were in the past expected to take the lead. Workers turned to the unions, but this could have jeopardised the unions. Now they can encourage workers to join other organisations which take up these issues. Some unions have done this. To link to the community organisations is not to sell out. The UDF can be used to fight issues that unions cannot directly fight.

The criticism has been made by some of the independent unions that the UDF is dominated by middle class people and that workers find it difficult to participate. The language used is English and workers can't compete with the debating skills of the middle classes.

It is true that the middle class tends to take over leadership and dominate community based organisations. The question is whether the working class can win genuine allies from the middle classes, for example intellectuals. Workers must join not only to give the UDF numbers but also direction; to make their voice heard. Where possible workers must also assume positions of leadership. The challenge for the UDF is whether it can evolve effective democratic processes to enable every constituent organisation to participate in the running of all the affairs of the front.

The criticism is also made that decisions are taken and then put to meetings for ratification, not for discussion.

Whilst it is true that we are not without shortcomings, some of the criticisms come out of ignorance. People who do not take part in the UDF cannot know who took the decisions because they were not at the meetings. If workers are not there the decisions will be taken by those who are present. But once they join they will decide. Where the democratic processes are not followed the workers will ask, "who took that decision?"

If the unions came into the UDF they could take up the programme of action and participate in the way they want to, but for the time being those in the UDF will decide issues.

At the national launching of the UDF some unions affiliated and others decided not to affiliate but nevertheless gave their support. This suggests that the support for the UDF is very wide amongst the independent unions, but that there are differences over the best way of giving support. Why do you feel that the unions should formally affiliate to the UDF?

Resistance to the constitutional proposals and the Koornhof Bills should not be restricted to one class. It is not merely workers who are affected but a combination of people; of classes. If the UDF creates a wider unity then the unions should join.

Some unions have said that joining the UDF may have devisive effects within their organisations because their members have differing political affiliations. It is also argued that the fact that some unions have joined and others have not is making union unity more difficult.

We have not made any union join. Every union will consider whether or not to join and the democratic processes within the unions will take their course.

The disunity amongst the unions is disappointing. We sent a letter to the feasibility committee giving our solidarity to the unions in their search for unity. We also stated that workers must be organised beyond the factory and need to form an alliance with other classes and that the UDF is the best forum for this.

It seems then that there are a number of possible ways in which workers could join the UDF: they could join as individuals or through their unions joining or through a federation of unions joining. Why in fact does the UDF see it as necessary for unions to become members?

The problem with a loose affiliation is that it is not easy to co-ordinate and to mobilise people. The situation would be greatly improved if unity on the factory floor and unity in the communities could be achieved. Combining unity at both these levels would greatly enhance the struggle. It would be easier to take decisions and to take action if the trade unions had already formed themselves into a single federation.

Appendix 5

CUSA on Political Organisations

The General Secretary of The Council of Unions of South Africa sent this resolution to the SALB (South African Labour Bulletin) in response to a request for a statement on its position in relation to political organisations.

During March and August this year the CUSA office had received a request from the National Forum Committee (NFC) and the United Democratic Front (UDF) and one other agency for its views and commitment on the Constitutional Proposals.

The three requests were put to the National Executive Committee during April. It was agreed that the matter be discussed at the Joint Executive Council (JEC) of CUSA on 30 April 1983.

The requests together with a draft resolution was prepared for the JEC meeting. A lengthy debate took place on various aspects. Amongst other issues discussed were the following:
1. the nature and philosophy of the organisations requesting the commitment;
2. the content of the CUSA response in the resolution;
3. the commitment CUSA was able to provide, and
4. the nature and content of the Constitutional Proposals.

The following resolution was then unanimously adopted:

"Having examined the proposals of the regime on the constitution;

Having further examined the basis of the call by various organisations regarding the constitutional proposals;

Noting that the Nationalist Party is presently in disarray and that these proposals may therefore be changed to impose white rule under different guise even through a referendum;

Knowing that the white opposition forces and parties are themselves divided and without any effect.

The Council of Unions of South Africa now therefore:
- wishes to place on record its complete and total rejection to the proposal;
- pledges itself to participate in every forum to work towards the achievement of a just and democratic society;
- calls upon its members to lend their individual support to all efforts of community organisations to end this foolish plan;
- pledges itself to all forces and all efforts to work towards a common citizenship in an undivided democratic and just society."

Following the response of various unions and the nature of press reports together with intransigent positions adopted by some sections of the communty CUSA is involved currently on an ongoing examination of its attitude and role in the UDF and the NFC.

Appendix 6

Labour Movement Relations with South African Trade Unions

Statement by the National Executive Committee of the British Labour Party, February 1983

The 1970s saw a major change in the South African political economy. The decade witnessed the development of a rapidly expanding, well organised non-racial (but predominantly African) trade union movement. The movement, although viewed with considerable suspicion and on occasions viciously attacked, now appears to have established itself as a permanent feature of the South African scene.

At the 1981 Labour Party Conference a resolution was unanimously adopted calling

". . . for the Labour Party, working with our trade union colleagues, to provide assistance and training to the independent, non-racial trade union movement in South Africa".

We must work towards finding the most appropriate way of implementing this resolution.

The first task is to distinguish those trade unions that can genuinely be considered to be 'independent and non-racial' from those that are not. The unions affiliated to the South African Confederation of Labour, organising white workers in openly racist unions, clearly fails to meet these criteria.

Unions affiliated to the Trade Union Council of South Africa, although organising some 170,000 Asian and Coloured workers as well as over 20,000 African workers, also cannot be accepted. Since its foundation in 1954 TUCSA has vacillated over the organisation of African workers. TUCSA first excluded African workers, then admitted them (1963), then finally expelled them (1969). In 1974, with the growth of African trade unions, TUCSA allowed Africans to affiliate, but generally organised them in exclusively African trade unions, in parallel to existing TUCSA unions. TUCSA's changing stance should be seen as the result of the growth and militancy of the independent non-racial trade unions, which threatened TUCSA's credibility as a major trade union federation.

TUCSA's African unions are highly bureaucratic, relying organisationally on their parent unions for finance and administration. Many general secretaries of the parallel unions are also the general secretaries of the registered parent trade unions. For these reasons, TUCSA unions cannot be considered to be 'independent'. In addition it must be noted that they are frequently brought into a firm with the co-operation of management to head off a recruitment drive by one of the independent non-racial trade unions. The attitude of the parent unions to the unionisation of African workers is one of paternalism and their commitment to workers' education and shop-floor democracy is non-existent.

The remaining unions can generally be described as non-racial, since they organise all workers in an industry. To date this has generally meant that they unionise African, Coloured and Asian workers, but their constitutions are non-racial, and once white workers are willing to join the unions they will be welcomed into membership. One union affiliated to the Federation of South African Trade Unions (FOSATU) recently made something of a breakthrough in recruiting some white workers into membership at a car plant, but clearly there is a long way to go before this becomes a significant trend.

The non-racial unions are also characterised by a commitment to participatory democracy so that the membership have a direct say in the policies and practises of their union. In addition, most have built considerable links with other community based organisations, co-operating on issues such as rents and bus fares, while in return receiving support for their industrial action from the community.

Perhaps most importantly, these unions are increasingly taking united action. During the protests that followed the death in detention of the trade unionist Neil Aggett, the unions co-operated to bring out 100,000 workers in a protest stoppage. In August 1981 and April 1982 the unions met at a 'summit' to thrash out a common policy for the non-racial union movement — a process which is continuing.

There are a rapidly growing number of trade unions, but the best known and most representative are those groups around FOSATU, CUSA (the Council of Unions of South Africa) and unaffiliated unions such as the General Workers Union, the South African Allied Workers Union and the Food and Canning Workers Union.

If there is any doubt over the status of a union there should be consultations with the ICFTU, or the appropriate International Trade Secretariat. These bodies are in constant contact with the non-racial unions and well able to advise on the policies and problems of the unions.

If these are the unions that we can support (and the list is not exhaustive) and the criteria by which we can judge them (non-racial, independent), what kind of solidarity can we have with them?

Forms of Solidarity

1. Solidarity Action in Britain

The British Labour movement has a long history of campaigning against the repression and racism that characterises apartheid. The Labour movement supports United Nations sanctions against South Africa and unilateral steps to reduce the economic links between Britain and South Africa, as well as the development of a strong non-racial trade union movement in South Africa.

British unions can and do play a valuable role in assisting the non-racial unions in their struggles with South African management and the state.

i. South African trade unionists not infrequently fall foul of the regime's repressive laws. There are a wide range of measures — including pickets, publicity, messages of support etc — that can be taken in order to bring pressure to bear on the South African authorities to secure the unionists' release.

ii. The hand of workers in disputes in South African subsidiaries of British companies can be substantially strengthened if British unions take action on their behalf. In the last few years, several examples of such action have taken place. For instance, in 1981, at the request of the ICFTU and after shop-floor meetings at the British Leyland plant at Cowley, Alex Kitson and Terry Duffy of TGWU and AUEW respectively met senior BL management in order to put pressure on the company during a strike at the BL plant in Cape Town. The intervention was successful, and subsequently many of the Cape Town workers were re-employed at the plant.

2. Material Assistance

Financial and material assistance have been supplied to the non-racial trade unions by the ICTFU, the TUC and a number of International Trade Secretariats for a number of years. The form that such assistance should take can best be determined in consultation with the independent and non-racial unions, but the following forms of assistance may be appropriate:

a. financial assistance for trade union education in South Africa;
b. scholarships for South African trade unionists;
c. collections for workers on strike and for the families of jailed or victimised workers;
d. subsidies for salaries of organisers and for office and transport equipment.

The ban on FOSATU receiving such funds has caused some difficulties, but these have not generally proved to be insuperable, with the international Labour movement supporting a wide range of educational and organisational projects in South Africa.

3. Visits to Britain

An increasing number of non-racial union representatives are visiting Britain to attend meetings with their trade union colleagues in this country. While contacts with racist trade unionists must of course be discouraged, contacts with representatives of the non-racial trade union movement assist in the establishment of a real rapport between unions.

These contacts have proved invaluable during disputes when solidarity must be based on an in-depth knowledge of the organisations and personalities involved.

4. Visits to South Africa

As the independent and non-racial unions have grown in strength they have come increasingly to value their links with the international Labour movement. Many union representatives now travel overseas and a number of British unions have received invitations from their South African counterparts. In particular, non-racial unions in disputes have at times felt that a visit by members of the international Labour movement would assist their cause.

At the same time it must be recognised that the South African government would, on occasion, welcome such visits, since they could be portrayed as breaking the policy of boycotting South Africa. Certainly the regime will be at pains to extract any propaganda value that it can from such visits.

It is therefore essential that any visit should only take place after consultations with the appropriate non-racial trade union, the TUC and the appropriate International Trade Secretariat.

Some guidance has been provided by those FOSATU unions affiliated to the International Metalworkers Federation. They suggested the following:

"We strongly favour fraternal contact between workers in South Africa and workers in other countries, at all levels, provided this is guided by the interests and requirements of workers. Visits to South Africa and visits overseas should be based on the concrete needs of workers. Visits should involve not only top officials, but also plant-based worker representatives.

"The aim of these visits should be to strengthen fraternal ties between organised workers in different countries and to carry forward the struggle for workers in South Africa to win the same rights as have been won by workers in other countries.

"Several visits to and from our unions have already taken place with shop stewards and union officials from Europe visiting unions and factories in South Africa and shop stewards and officials from our unions travelling to the USA and Europe. This contact has been valuable and will be encouraged in the future, provided it takes place in accordance with the above principles and guidelines" (Press Release, 22 October 1981).

These guidelines can be elaborated upon by suggesting that:
 i. visits should *only* take place at the request of and according to a schedule drawn up in co-operation between British unions and the independent and non-racial trade unions in South Africa;
 ii. emphasis should be given to company-based contacts, i.e. the exchange of visits by trade union representatives working for the same parent company in Britain and South Africa;
 iii. British unions should specifically refrain from going on visits to South Africa organised by the South African government (or its front line organisations) or by companies with interests in South Africa;
 iv. great care should be taken in making any statement to the media concerning the visit.

If these guidelines are followed, visits to South Africa can be undertaken and the solidarity so vital to the international Labour movement can be strengthened.

Note: In drawing up this document consultations were held with the following organisations:

International Confederation of Free Trade Unions
Trades Union Congress

International Metalworkers Federation
International Transport Workers Federation
International Union of Food and Allied Workers Associations
South African Congress of Trade Unions
African National Congress
Anti-Apartheid Movement
Council of Unions of South Africa
Federation of South African Trade Unions

Appendix 7

International Policy Statement adopted by FOSATU Central Committee, April 1984

FOSATU believes in international worker contact in order to pursue the following goals:

1. To build international worker solidarity in the struggle against the economic, social and political oppression of workers.
2. To build effective worker organisation to counter and reduce the power of the multinational corporations (MNCs).
3. To support workers' struggles in other countries in whatever way FOSATU can.
4. To ensure that the institutions of the international trade union movement are not being used by anti-worker forces to create divisions and a loss of independence within the South African worker movement.
5. To assist in increasing the international condemnation of and pressure on the present racist regime in South Africa.

FOSATU realises that the pursuit of these general goals requires the carrying out of a wide range of activities. These activities are not without their difficulties and problems. FOSATU accordingly sets out the following guidelines on activities related to each of the four goals.

1. *International Worker Solidarity:*
   FOSATU understands by this fraternal support to generally strengthen independent worker organisation in all countries. In particular at present the focus is on the following in the South African situation.
   1.1 Financial assistance — to build independent worker organisation in South Africa has required and will continue to require financial assistance from the international trade union movement. FOSATU sees three stages through which our organisation will go in the receipt of such financial assistance.

   The first was financial assistance in the general operating expenses of both affiliates and the federation. The second is one where affiliates are self-sufficient in regard to general running expenses whilst the federation receives assistance to build structures and facilities of benefit to affiliates. The third stage is where both affiliates and the federation are self-sufficient in regard to general running expenses and financial assistance will be for extraordinary projects to further develop the worker movement.

   FOSATU believes that financial assistance is fundamental to international worker solidarity. However, it can be a double-edged sword that can build or destroy. Financial assistance must not be used to creat dependency and division within the South African worker movement.

1.2 International travel — where and when this is possible there is no doubt that it is important for building fraternal links. The chance to meet and talk to fraternal unionists outside South Africa will educate our leadership in the common problems of the working class.

FOSATU believes that such travel should be seen as part of a systematic programme of study, research and working activity. Those going must be appropriately briefed on the nature of their visit and must submit written reports upon their return. FOSATU should wherever appropropriate finance its own independent travel to build fraternal links.

However, it must not be forgotten that overseas support cannot replace organisation at home. FOSATU's purpose is to educate its leadership and to establish effective worker solidarity. Fraternal visits to South Africa by worker leadership from abroad, arranged within the framework of FOSATU policy on such visits, can also be of great value, especially since it can involve larger number of workers than the limited number who will get the opportunity to travel abroad themselves.

1.3 Expertise and Information — the worker struggle in South Africa can benefit greatly from the hard lessons learnt overseas. In many areas, such as Health and Safety, great expertise has been developed. Here in South Africa we must make use of this rather than try and learn it all again.

FOSATU believes that such knowledge must be exchanged both by visits overseas and more particularly by people coming to South Africa where they can have greater contact with shop stewards and officials.

However, FOSATU is fully aware of the fact that we have to develop skills here that will allow us to effectively use such information in our circumstances.

1.4 Publications — FOSATU should actively circulate its publications so as to inform people what is happening here. Likewise we must obtain foreign publications so as to get more information on worker problems elsewhere in the world. This is necessary because of the anti-worker propaganda that the press, radio and TV call news here in South Africa.

2. *Multinational Corporations (MNC):*
FOSATU believes that the MNCs have excessive power which is used to the detriment of workers both in South Africa and in the home countries of these MNCs. We believe it is in the common interest of all workers that organisation is strong in all places where the MNCs operate. FOSATU's experience has shown that as a minimum, strong factory-based organisation around a Shop Steward movement and active membership is needed to counter the power of capital and the MNCs in particular.

2.1 FOSATU accordingly believes that effective worker solidarity in the struggle against the MNCs depends on contact at all levels —

membership, Shop Stewards, the union and the ITS. Worker solidarity will not be built on the basis of contact at one or two of these levels only.

2.2 FOSATU will initiate and join any positive attempt to build international organisation within each multinational. FOSATU believes that the bringing together of Shop Stewards (or their equivalent) is the key element to such organising efforts and in this way the whole union can be fully integrated into this bitter struggle.

FOSATU believes that such organisation can build up an active exchange of information and can work toward common demands on wages and working conditions.

2.3 FOSATU believes that it should begin to establish greater direct contact with workers in MNCs in so-called Third World countries which share many similar problems to those experienced here.

3. *Vigilance Against Division and Loss of Independence*

FOSATU believes that the institutions of the international trade union movement are still bedevilled by the politics of international power and the 'Cold War' and that this is to the lasting detriment of workers. FOSATU's own experience makes it wary of the dangers of division and organisational collapse that arise out of many of the practices of these institutions.

FOSATU believes that we have to guard against being caught in the web of international politics rather than building effective worker solidarity.

3.1 FOSATU accordingly believes that there must be clear control over and policies towards the access of international financial assistance. The dangers of such finance have already been seen in South Africa — it props up non-existent unions, creates disunity and can be used for particular political purposes rather than to assist in the development of trade unions.

FOSATU believes that the unco-ordinated and unchecked access by affiliates to financial assistance will create a decline in organisation and potential division. FOSATU favours assistance through co-ordinated channels and within a clear programme to move the three stages outlined in point 1.1 above.

3.2 Likewise we believe in a co-ordinated approach on the side of the donor organisations. This will have two important practical effects for us in South Africa.

Firstly, differences of opinion and interest between them will have to be solved overseas in meetings instead of creating problems here in South Africa. Secondly, FOSATU (and other S.A. unions) will be able to more effectively deal with one multilateral effort rather than waste energy and resources on dealing with a number of different efforts.

3.3 This multilateral effort should deal with the requirements of general solidarity as dealt with in 1.1 above. Within this, affiliates can and should — in consultation with FOSATU — establish relationships with unions overseas for the purposes of more specific and detailed solidarity projects and the funding of these.

3.4 FOSATU accepts the principle of co-ordinating councils in South Africa of the affiliates of a particular ITS. Such co-ordinating councils should not be a vehicle for propping up splinter unions and giving credibility to the anti-worker and racist practises of certain trade unions in South Africa.

3.5 FOSATU believes that because of their particular political interests governments should not interfere in the affairs of the international trade union movement and accordingly would prefer to conduct its affairs directly with trade union and labour organisations.

3.6 FOSATU is of the view that affiliation to the ICFTU, WCL or WFTU would not be of significant advantage to FOSATU membership and workers in S.A. at present. The particular position in South Africa would make any such affiliation politically complicated and prevent a full and active participation in all activities of these organisations. FOSATU accordingly believes that only one unified national centre should affiliate to such international organisations.

4. *International Pressure on South Africa:*
   FOSATU has continually stated its implacable opposition to South Africa's racist regime and, therefore, fully supports international pressure on South Africa to bring about social justice and a truly democratic society.

4.1 Because of the specific problems of the South African situation FOSATU believes that visits by trade unionists to South Africa should only be made on the specific request or arrangement of the independent non-racial trade unions in South Africa. FOSATU believes that other visits are used by the South African government to gain credibility for its actions both within and outside the country.

4.2 For similar reasons FOSATU is opposed to the stationing of permanent representatives of the international trade union movement and related organisations inside South Africa.

4.3 FOSATU as a trade union organisation concerned with the jobs and livelihood of its members has to give careful consideration to the question of disinvestment. However, it is FOSATU's considered view that the pressure for disinvestment has had a positive effect and should therefore not be lessened. FOSATU is definitely opposed to foreign investment that accepts the conditions of oppression maintained by this regime.

   FOSATU is, however, also clear that its own focus of attention must be the building of a strong worker movement in South Africa that can set the terms of foreign investment and ultimately ensure that the factories, machines and buildings presently in South Africa will be retained in South Africa to the ultimate benefit of all.

Appendix 8

Making Contact with Black Unions in South Africa

It is easy to write or telephone to unions in South Africa. Some even have a telex operation. All welcome messages of support and solidarity. Postal censorship exists in South Africa but most letters do not get opened. In the following list of addresses you should be able to find how to contact all the major South African unions. Remember that few have a centralised head office and that branch offices and locals play a more important role. The head office of the FOSATU federation, for example, is a small office in a Cape Town suburb. If you wanted to find out information about FOSATU it would be better to contact their publishing centre situated in their regional office in Durban.

FOSATU

FOSATU Head Office
2 Goodhope Street
7530 Bellville South   Tel: 021-951412

FOSATU Affiliates Head Offices:
Chemical Workers Industrial
Union (CWIU)
Suite 3, Central Court
61 Hime Street
4052 JACOBS   Tel: 031-67401/482633

National Sugar Industry Employees Union (NSIEU)
216 Goodhope Centre
92 Queen Street
4001 DURBAN   Tel: 031-65563

National Union of Textile Workers (NUTW)
5 Central Court
125 Gale Street
4001 DURBAN   Tel: 031-65250

Metal and Allied Workers Union (MAWU)
14 Fines Building
Voortrekker Street
1500 BENONI   Tel: 011-543388

Paper, Wood and Allied Workers Union (PWAWU)
2 Palladium Building
1560 SPRINGS   Tel: 011-567925

Sweet, Food and Allied Workers Union (SFAWU)
3 Central Court
125 Gale Street
4001 DURBAN   Tel: 031-337350

Transport and General Workers Union (TGWU)
First Floor
Harrister House
65 Harrison Street
JOHANNESBURG 2001   Tel: 011-8364463

Jewellers and Goldsmiths Unions (JGU)
201/4 City Centre
18 Corporation Street
8001 CAPE TOWN   Tel: 021-468086

National Automobile and Allied Workers Union (NAAWU)
102 Lotus Building
Cottrell Street
PORT ELIZABETH 6001   Tel: 041-46010/9

**REGIONAL OFFICES OF
FOSATU AND AFFILIATES**

EASTERN PROVINCE
9 Lotus Building
Cottrell Street
PORT ELIZABETH 6001   Tel: 041-414026

NATAL
Shop 12
12 Webbers Centre
HAMMARSDALE 3700   Tel: 0325-61665

NORTHERN NATAL
1 Waste Centre
37 Morris Street
EMPANGENI RAIL 3910   Tel: 0351-21673

TRANSVAAL
30 World Centre
48 Railway Street   Tel: 011-8256222
1401 GERMISTON   011-518818

WESTERN PROVINCE
2 Goodhope Street
BELLVILLE SOUTH 7530   Tel: 021-951412

FOSATU LOCALS

NATAL

DURBAN   Tel: TGWU — 031-319511
2/3/5 Central Court   MAWU — 031-312565
125 Gale Street   SFAWU — 031-337350
4001 DURBAN   NUTW — 031-65250

HAMMARSDALE
Shop 12 Webbers Shopping Centre
3700 HAMMARSDALE   Tel: NUTW — 0325-61665

ISIPINGO
6 Jadwat Building   Shop 8
148 Old Main Road   Isipingo Mall
4110 ISIPINGO   100 Old Main Road
Tel: MAWU/CWIU —   4110 ISIPINGO
031-923780   Tel: NAAWU — 031-924190

JACOBS   Tel: CWIU — 031-486648
Suite 3, 61 Hime Street   MAWU/PWAWU
4052 JACOBS   031-482633

PIETERMARITZBURG
Suite 106
518 Church Street   Tel: 0331-26121 (SFAWU)
PIETERMARITZBURG 3201   -24596 (FOSATU)

PINETOWN   Tel: 031-729766 (FOSATU)
9 Imperial Lane   -711663 (NUTW)
3600 PINETOWN   -725424 (MAWU)

NORTHERN NATAL   Tel: 0351-21994 (CWIU)
1 Waste Centre Building   -24381 (MAWU)
37 Morris Street   -25823 (PWAWU)
EMPANGENI RAIL 3910   -23500 (TGWU)

TRANSVAAL

BENONI

7 Fines Building   Tel: 011-540337
Voortrekker Street   -548013
1500 BENONI   -543663

GERMISTON
30 World Centre   Tel: 011-8251916 (MAWU)
48 Railway Street   -8256826 (CWIU)
1401 GERMISTON   -518818 (NUTW)

JOHANNESBURG
First Floor
Harrister House
65 Harrison Street
2001 JOHANNESBURG   Tel: 011-8364736

KATLEHONG
Morena Store
Black Reef Road
1832 KATLEHONG   Tel: 011-8653500

KEMPTON PARK
Shop 11 Westblou
48 West Street
1628 KEMPTON PARK   Tel: 011-9755876

PRETORIA NORTH
10/11 Penor Building
Cnr. Gerrit Maritz &
    West Streets
PRETORIA NORTH 0166   Tel: 012-551650/552328

SPRINGS
1/2/18 Palladium Building   P.O. Box 154
Third Avenue   1563 Kwa Thema
1560 SPRINGS   Tel: 011-566215 (SFAWU)
                                            -566826

VEREENIGING
39 Beaconsfield Ave.   P.O. Box 865
VEREENIGING   VEREENIGING
1930   1930
                             Tel: 016-224362

CUSA

CUSA Head Office
7th Floor
Lekton House
5 Wanderers Street
JOHANNESBURG 2001   Tel: 011-298031

CUSA Affiliates

Building, Construction and Allied Workers Union
Head Office   **Branches**
P.O. Box 10928   DURBAN
JOHANNESBURG   Tel: 031-31-9707
2000   PIETERMARITZBURG
Tel: 011-23-8302   Tel: 0331-5-4642
                           PORT ELIZABETH
                           Tel: 041-41-3403
                           PRETORIA
                           Tel: 012-26-6242

Food Beverage Workers Union
P.O. Box 25271
FERREIRASDORP 2048   Tel: 011-23-8357

Hotel Liquor and Catering Trade Employees Union
P.O. Box 1409
JOHANNESBURG 2000   Tel: 011-836-4738

National Union of Mineworkers
P.O. Box 10928
JOHANNESBURG 2000   Tel: 011-29-4561

S.A. Chemical Workers Union
P.O. Box 4990
JOHANNESBURG 2000   Tel: 011-29-8920

South African Laundry, Dry Cleaning and Dyeing Workers Union
P.O. Box 25271
FERRAIRASDORP 2000   Tel: 011-23-9058

Steel Engineering and Allied Workers Union of S.A.
P.O. Box 61289
MARSHALLTOWN 2017   Tel: 011-834-4771

S.A. Black Municipality and Allied Workers
P.O. Box 23027
Joubert Park 2044   Tel: 011-29-8507

Textile Workers Union — Transvaal
P.O. Box 10488
JOHANNESBURG 2000   Tel. 011-37-6591

Transport and Allied Workers Union
P.O. Box 4469   **Branches**
JOHANNESBURG 2000   DURBAN
Tel: 011-29-4784   Tel: 031-6-0464
                                      PORT ELIZABETH
                                      Tel: 041-4-5448

United African Motor Workers Union
514 Willie Theron Building   **Branch:**
Bosman Street,   DURBAN
PRETORIA 0002   Tel: 031-6-1105
Tel: 012-323-0838

UNAFFILIATED UNIONS

Black Allied Workers Union
P.O. Box 2691
DURBAN 4000   Tel: 031-311516

Black Allied Mining and Construction Workers
Abbey House
51 Commissioner Street
JOHANNESBURG 2001
Tel: 011 834 6681/2

Black Municipal Workers Union
P.O. Box 23027
Joubert Park 2044   Tel: 011-239017

Cape Town Municipal Workers Association
P.O. Box 49
ATHLONE 770   Tel: 021-678140

Commercial Catering and Allied Workers Union of S.A.
P.O. Box 7135
JOHANNESBURG 2000   Tel: 011-23-6127/8/9

Food and Canning Workers Union
P.O. Box 2678
CAPE TOWN 8000   Tel: 021-46-6066/7

General and Allied Workers Union
P.O. Box 6914
JOHANNESBURG 2000   Tel: 011-838-2377

General Workers Union
Benbow Building
3 Beverley Street
ATHLONE 7764   Tel: 021-670870

Media Workers Association of S.A.
P.O. Box 11136
JOHANNESBURG 2000   Tel: 011-29-8005

Motor Assembly Components Workers Union
P.O. Box 2924
PORT ELIZABETH 6000   Tel: 041-54-4245

Municipal and General Workers Union
2nd Floor
Chancellor House
25 Fox Street
JOHANNESBURG 2001   Tel: 011-836-6025

Orange-Vaal General Workers Union
308 Trevor Building
Voortrekker Street
VEREENIGING 1930   Tel: 016-224743

South African Allied Workers Union (SAAWU)
94 Tasmin Centre   East London Office
122 Victoria Street   PO Box 7002
DURBAN 4001   East London 5200
Tel: 031-69217   Tel: 0431-26-899